76-735

76-735

796.93   Auran, John Henry
Aur
         The ski better book

DATE DUE		
DEC 20	NOV 18	

North Junior High Library
St. Cloud, Minnesota

Other Books by John Auran

America's Ski Book (Editor)
Ski Down the Years (Contributor)
Skiing Is a Family Sport

skiing from the edges up

john henry auran
senior editor, skiing magazine
& jerry winter

The Dial Press
New York
1975

North Junior High Library
St. Cloud, Minnesota

76-735

Library of Congress Cataloging in Publication Data

Auran, John Henry.
The ski better book.

Includes index.
1. Skis and skiing. I. Winter, Jerry, 1944– joint author. II. Title.
GV854.A92   796.9'3   75-19141
ISBN 0–8037–7617–9 ; 8096-6 (pbk.)

Copyright © 1975 by John Henry Auran and Gerald A. Winter

All rights reserved
No part of this book may be reproduced in any form or by any means without the prior written permission of the Publisher, excepting brief quotes used in connection with reviews written specifically for inclusion in a magazine or newspaper.

Manufactured in the United States of America

First printing

Acknowledgments

Drawings by Alfred Avison. Photographs by Malcolm Reiss, except those on the following pages: Aspen Skiing Corporation, Aspen, Colo.: 79, 73. John Auran: 8. Austrian National Tourist Office: 99. Boise Basin, Idaho: 105. Adrian Bouchard; 2 top. Jan Brunner: 11. Gray Rocks Inn, Ltd., Quebec, Canada: 103. Killington Ski Area, Killington, Vt.: 4 bottom. Fred Lindholm: 76. Mt. Tom Ski Area, Holyoke, Mass.: 102. Norwegian Information Service: 95. Rossignol Ski Co.: 39. Schussland: 72. *Skiing* Magazine: 43, 44. Ski Tül: 85. Snowmass Resort, Snowmass, Colo.: 111. Stratton Corporation, Stratton, Vt.: bottom frontispiece. Virginia Sturgess: 84, 86, 88. Sun Valley, Sun Valley, Idaho: center frontispiece, 2 bottom, 4 top, 54, 77, 90 top. Swiss National Tourist Office: 9, 71, 74, 75, 90 bottom, 109. Vail Associates, Inc., Vail Colo.: 107. Waterville Valley, Waterville Valley, N. H.: 3, 14.

Special thanks to Daniel Mornet of the Rossignol Ski Company for demonstrating for Malcolm Reiss's photography and to *Skiing* Magazine for use of its archives.

	Introduction	1
1	Mileage: Practicing What You Learn	7
2	From the Edges Up	13
3	Balance: The Means to an End	27
4	Equipment	33
5	Turn Initiation	47
6	Getting the Turn and Yourself Together	57
7	Terrain and Snow Conditions	69
8	Psyching Up for Skiing	79
9	Ski Maintenance	83
10	The Uses of Racing and Cross-Country Skiing	89
11	If It's White and Slippery, Ski on It!	101
	Index	115

Skiing is going through its most exciting period of change since steel edges were put on skis nearly fifty years ago. Skis have become shorter and easier to handle. Boots are more comfortable and functional. Better bindings provide a greater margin of safety. Beginners can now learn in a week what used to take a season or more of arduous apprenticeship to master. And at the outer limits of performance, racers and freestylers are widening the sport's horizon with maneuvers that were never dreamed of just a few years ago.

I am one of the fortunate few who was put on skis not long after I could walk. If I went through snowplow, stem christie, and parallel turn stages as I learned, I do not remember them. Even many years later, when I was aware there were such things, it never seriously occurred to me to analyze skiing in those terms. I simply skied. It wasn't until I started writing about skiing fifteen years ago that I suddenly became aware how troublesome and confusing *learning* to ski really is.

I wish I could claim that I saw the solution to all the problems of struggling skiers in one blinding flash, but it wasn't as simple as that. Editing how-to-ski articles, at first I only had a feeling that there was a gap between theory and practice, that there was something that

---

Expert skiing from three eras: These photos, taken about ten years apart, show how approach and technique have changed since the 1950s. As equipment improved, skiers were able to ski more erect, relaxed, and with less upper-body motion. It's also evident that they've become much more aggressive in the way they tackle their turns.

Introduction

ski instructors weren't telling. That feeling gradually grew into conviction after studying thousands of technique sequences that demonstrated to me that instructors and some of the leading technique experts were frequently claiming to do one thing and actually doing another. This wasn't easy to detect. Keep in mind, this was the era when the *right* length of ski was from the floor to the wrist of your upstretched hand. The idea that beginners might be better off with something shorter and less cumbersome was still relatively new. It was a time when skiers were judged by the type of turn they made: snowplow—novice; stem turn and stem christies—intermediate; parallel turn—advanced; shortswing (short, continuous parallel turns)—expert.

There was a mighty feud at that time, too, between the followers of the Austrian instruction method, who counter-rotated (reverse shoulder in the vernacular) and those of the French method, who rotated their shoulders in the direction of the turn. It was more than obvious that you could ski both ways, and well, despite proclamations from both sides that "you can't ski that way!" Despite much thundering about the "irrefutable laws of physics," none

---

Until the early 1960s, slalom racers did a good deal of skiing with their skis perfectly parallel and with virtually no daylight between their legs, and a whole generation of skiers wore themselves out trying to do likewise. Then racers broadened their stance and started using their legs independently (unparallel) and found they could go even faster with more security. It was almost a decade before instructors and skiers followed suit.

The Ski Better Book 2

High-backed boots, which came into vogue in the late 1960s, provided skiers with greatly improved edge control and freedom of movement. They also provided a means of recovery from sitting back not available before. This development created a whole new breed, called freestylers or hot-doggers, who are performing stunts considered impossible ten years ago.

of the experts I encountered could satisfactorily explain why it was possible to turn the shoulders in two different and opposite directions and still achieve the same results.

Although this particular dispute is no longer an issue, its basis—the confusion between cause and effect—continues to linger. The situation has improved greatly, but ski schools are still excessively concerned with how you look executing a particular maneuver instead of your mastery of the fundamentals that are involved. As a result, there is a needless profusion of teaching methods—American Teaching Method (ATM), Graduated Length Method (GLM), Austrian, French, etc.—and lack of clarity about what the aspiring skier should be told. The many labels that have been put on skiers who have survived the novice phase over the years—improving intermediate, stem christie skier, beginning parallel, among many others—are only a hint of the ambivalence that is still haunting ski instruction and the afflicted skiers themselves.

It was slightly unhinging at the time to find myself unclassified and not quite fitting any prescribed models. Good parallel turns, the fashion of the day demanded, had to be made with skis and legs squeezed closely together. Per-

sonally, I wasn't bothered that I had three or four inches of daylight showing, but I was put off that I should be considered less proficient for *that* reason, particularly as I invariably did about as well in the tough going as some of the technique gurus who were insisting it should be done by their book. It occurred to me that organized ski instruction was, perhaps unwittingly, playing games by arbitrarily prescribing the model and then arbitrarily putting me down when I failed to match it. If it was happening to me, it was bound to be happening to other skiers.

The Parallel Turn Has Died

This realization was only the first step toward enlightenment. There seemed to be something ski instructors were not telling us or did not know. What was it? Yet, regardless of my own feelings, people *were* being taught to ski. How was that accomplished? Among the avant-garde, things were being done that were, according to the conventional wisdom of the time, wrong if not impossible. Why was it possible? And what, if anything, did this mean to the less skillful skiers?

The answers to these questions did not come in one flash, but rather in bits

---

No wonder learning to ski used to be tough. Compare the mid-1930s skier's equipment with that of the young woman getting a modern-style lesson. Short skis and better boots have sparked an instructional revolution—still going on—that makes skiing quicker and easier to learn.

The Ski Better Book 4

and pieces from hundreds of different people and events. There were encounters with such visionaries as short-ski advocate Clif Taylor, and direct-to-parallel prophet Walter Foeger. I had discussions with racing analysts such as Warren Witherell and hints from hundreds of pragmatic instructors who pruned a bit here and simplified some more there. I argued with the old guard and endured hours of technical explanations from the designers of new skis and boots. Every so often, a well-put question from one of my readers posed something I took for granted in a new light.

I doubt very much if I could have put it all together if it had not been for my colleague, Doug Pfeiffer, who battled the instruction establishment for many years as a maverick ski school director in California and Colorado, and who continued the battle from behind a desk at **Skiing** Magazine. Over the years, we must have spent thousands of hours arguing and analyzing technique, instruction, and equipment and the effects of one on the others.

I would venture to guess there was no wrinkle, however outlandish, that we did not explore at one time or another. Doug is a true expert and, at heart, a born teacher, while I am inclined to be a bomb thrower. But no matter how outrageous some of my ideas, Doug patiently played devil's advocate to see if there might be something to them.

It was during one of these sessions about two years ago that, out of the blue, I suggested an article that was to be called "The Parallel Turn Has Died; We've Come To Bury It." It was a ridiculous idea, meant only for a chuckle, yet Doug persisted: "We no longer ski parallel?"

"No, not exactly," I reasoned. "But the parallel turn with legs close together and all the other nonsense that went with it is gradually being phased out of skiing. Parallel *per se* is no longer the badge of skiing accomplishment and expertise. Even first-time ski-weekers are doing them and I have not heard anyone tell me to put my knees together in several years. In fact, the whole structure of ski school drills that was gospel a few years ago is collapsing like a house of cards."

Then sometime much later, another absurd idea came to me: "Then there's not much left for ski schools to teach."

"Well"—long pause by Doug—"there's still a hell of a lot for skiers to learn and someone has to teach it."

Somewhere during that night the basic ideas behind this book were born. Skiing, as I see it, is no longer a problem of getting started. Short-ski instruction has taken care of that. Nor is it the mastering of a series of maneuvers, since the decline of the parallel turn has demonstrated that a maneuver-oriented approach leads to a dead end. Rather, it is a matter of applying a few fundamentals to whatever curve balls the snow and surface of the mountains are throwing at you, whether it means your first attempting a steep slope, coping with a patch of blue ice, attacking a slalom course, or devising a freestyle routine.

It is not the purpose of this book to tell you how to become a racer or a hot-dogger, or any other kind of skier for that matter; it's up to you to find what gives you the most pleasure in skiing. Nor is it my purpose, despite occasional disparaging remarks, to replace your ski instructor. He, too, has changed and you will need him. Rather it is more of an invitation to look at skiing from a different, perhaps broader, perspective that makes the next step not an insurmountable obstacle, but rather another challenge to become a better skier.

I hope to present a true picture of the **forest** by avoiding these various pitfalls. And the proverbial **trees** of skiing nomenclature will not impair our clear view as we progress from the beginning, where the skis meet the snow at the edges, and analyze the problems which confront all skiers from the edges up.

One
Mileage: Practicing What You Learn

If the advice in this book had to be summed up in a sentence, it would have to be: **Get all the mileage you can.**

Mileage. Simply from the sound of it, you get the idea of what you have to do to become a good skier: put miles on your skis. As in any other sport, proficiency in skiing is achieved by practice. As a wise old instructor once put it, "There's no substitute for doing it."

Yet, strange as it seems, mileage as a concept, as a methodical way of achieving skiing competence, is relatively undeveloped in the sport, even in ski racing. As recently as the 1960s, slalom racers laboriously used to climb the hill for every run, both in training and during the race. The assumption was that the climb was good physical conditioning and good mental exercise for memorizing the complex gate combinations. It was not until the French head coach, Honoré Bonnet, trained his team with the aid of high-speed lifts that the absurdity of the old approach became apparent, especially in the race results.

Whereas racers used to run through sixty to eighty gates during an hour-and-a-half to two-hour practice session, under Bonnet's system they were running three times as many. And contrary to everyone's expectations, the French did not miss gates during the race. They ran the gates more aggressively and more smoothly than anyone had previously thought possible.

Obviously, the French racers were getting more miles per practice session than their rivals (until the latter did likewise), but they gained several other benefits, too. If a racer fell, missed a gate, or did something wrong, no real

Honoré Bonnet, former head of the French ski team, is an original thinker whose training ideas are just beginning to be applied to recreational skiing.

harm was done. Within minutes, the racer could be back at the top of the course to try again, with the source of his mistake still fresh in his mind. He felt free to experiment, again, because a temporary failure did not mean a loss of precious time. Perhaps most important, the racer did not have the opportunity to stew about the course and its various difficulties, instead learning to cultivate spontaneity, to react to conditions as he found them, rather than as he might have liked them to be.

Beyond the Maneuvers

Strangely, the importance of mileage remains one of the least appreciated aspects of skiing's French Revolution. Inspired by the success of the enigmatic French super-star, Jean-Claude Killy, those who skied for fun relatively quickly adopted French equipment and techniques to the point where their elements are today found even in the beginners' curriculum of most ski schools. But the same recreational skiers gave little thought to how the French achieved their competence. It is unfortunately still too common for ski instructors to spend more time lecturing and demonstrating to their students than letting them ski. Consequently, the skiers spend more time contemplating what they are going to do than doing it.

"Ah," I can hear you say, "I'm not a racer, just someone who is trying to get the hang of this game." My answer to

The Ski Better Book **8**

you is: If the very best skiers are able to ski better by increasing their mileage, surely so can you, regardless of whether you are a beginner trying to achieve intermediate status or an expert out to master the latest wrinkle in technique.

Basically, the idea behind skiing could not be simpler: to come down a mountain under control, you have to turn. Turning is to skiing what hitting the ball over the net is to tennis. But just as the object in tennis is not simply to bash the ball, but to direct it so that you can score a point, so in skiing the object is not simply to turn, but to turn under an infinite variety of snow conditions and terrain.

Unfortunately, a good deal of ski instruction *and* the way most skiers approach the sport conspire to prevent skiers from progressing beyond the mere mechanics of the turn to the vast range of challenge and excitement that skiing has to offer.

To use the tennis analogy once more: While they are deciding how to hold and angle the racket for a backhand, the ball is going by them.

Pitfalls New and Old

In the not-so-distant past, this problem was epidemic in skiing, dooming mil-

Ski school problem number one. Students stand around—not accumulating mileage—while the instructor demonstrates. This is, of course, necessary at various points during the lesson, but there's far too much of it, particularly in beginner classes. Fortunately, the situation is improving (see photo page 11) as the ski school curriculum is simplified.

9 Mileage: Practicing What You Learn

lions to permanent intermediate status. Although ATM and GLM instruction, with their almost direct approach to parallel skiing, are a vast improvement, some of the old pitfalls remain and new ones have been created.

There are still many instructors who drill and lecture to the point of making you so self-conscious about the incidental details of turning that you might as well be on a parade ground rather than a ski slope. The very fact that ski areas are going out of their way to spare novices as much agony as possible with specially designed and intensely groomed teaching slopes makes initiation to the sport possible without encountering ice, deep snow, bad weather, or any other hard-to-handle snow conditions. This is well and good up to a point, but it leaves you ill prepared for skiing without supervision and away from the teaching slope. The shock of discovering that you are not ready for more challenging and interesting aspects of skiing can make you mentally so defensive that progress becomes almost impossible and the value of the miles you accumulate is marginal at best.

Conceivably, you could stay in ski school until you are reasonably proficient, but cost aside, that is not the way it works out for most skiers. You need time on your own to absorb the material you have learned in your lessons. In any event, you will be eager to solo.

The Key

The key to becoming a better skier is to make your solo miles count by first coming to grips with the fundamentals and then cultivating spontaneity and going beyond the mere mechanics of turning.

Perhaps because skiing has been in almost constant technical turmoil since the end of World War I, when it became a popular participant sport, little thought has been given to the problems of skiers as they cut the ski-school apron strings.

Just about all available literature on how to ski is restricted to the execution of particular turns, with the admonition to practice, but without saying how. This is a book to redress the balance . . . by a skier who has had a lot of experience in getting better and who wishes dearly that he knew then what he knows now.

Be your turn ever so humble, keep moving—like the intrepid soul in the center of the picture. Inexperienced skiers frequently stop because they're self-conscious, or the turn didn't come off quite as they thought it should. This interrupts continuity and kills spontaneity. Unless you're tired or in danger, keep skiing as long as you can.

Skiing seems complicated because past technical limitations of boots and skis made it so. The complications persist because the traditional idea that you learn by going from snowplow to snowplow turn to stem christie, etc.—instead of mastering fundamentals—lingers on, both in ski schools and among skiers taught by the older methods. Today, tens of thousands are lesser skiers than they could be because their minds and reflexes have been boggled by technical irrelevancies.

Actually, skiing is quite simple if you will stop dreaming wishfully about parallel turns, **avalement** (a French word for the exciting-looking deep knee bend that results when you go over a big bump), or whatever the latest gimmick happens to be, and start thinking in terms of combining a handful of basic skiing skills to deal with whatever the mountain happens to throw at you. Understand these skills and you will quickly spot your weaknesses. Master them, and the maneuvers that seem so elusive now will come almost automatically.

A Purposeful But Temporary Omission

It is customary to talk first about balance and how to stand on your skis. On the hill that is the way it has to be. However, there are more fundamental reasons **why** we do **what** we do when we are on skis. With an understanding of these first, all the things that are done to stay in balance will make much more sense.

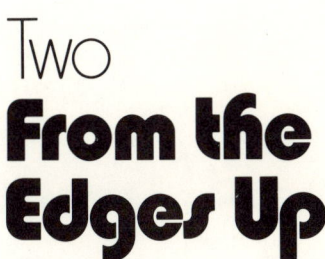

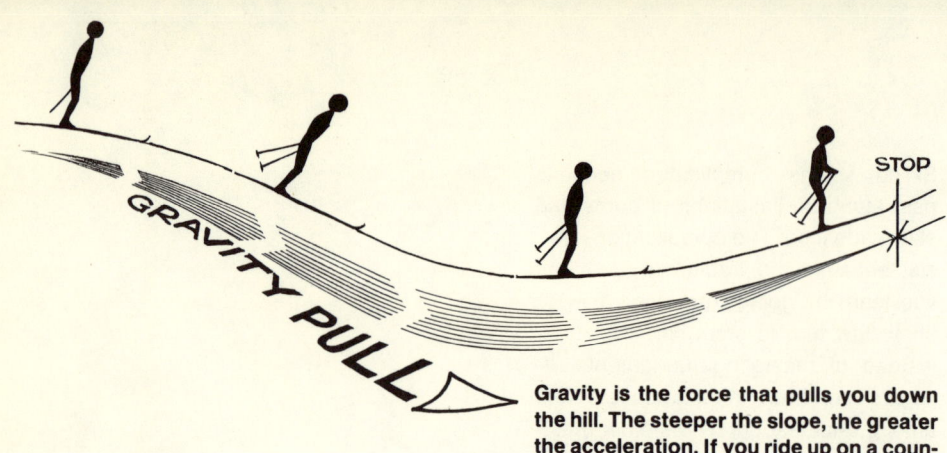

Gravity is the force that pulls you down the hill. The steeper the slope, the greater the acceleration. If you ride up on a counter-slope, you'll slow down and eventually stop. However, unless you do something about it, gravity will pull you backward until you reach the lowest part of the hill.

So I am skipping the topic of balance for now, although you may peek ahead to Chapter 3 if you prefer to keep things in *on-the-mountain* sequence.

Because skiing's fundamentals have been so badly neglected, let us start over at the very beginning.

Gravity, Centrifugal Force, and Friction

Nature provides the forces that make our skis slide down the hill and turn. Modern skis and boots are specifically designed to help us manage these forces. We use muscle power to manage the equipment.

Note especially the sequence of those three brief statements above. Too many inexperienced skiers consider skiing an awful struggle with the mountain and try to turn their skis—somehow—with brute muscle power. Nothing is more self-defeating. So as a start, let's look at the forces involved in skiing and, in subsequent chapters, how skis are used to manage these forces and how we manage the skis.

The Ski Better Book 14

The results of centrifugal force can be seen in the photo on the right. The racer has banked toward the inside to resist the force but this has the (desirable) effect of bending the skis and making the edge bite harder.

(1) Gravity, for our purposes, is the force that pulls us straight down the hill. When the hill steepens, we speed up; when it flattens, we slow down; and if we ski uphill we come to a stop.

When we allow the skis to go straight down the hill without any attempts to turn, the skis follow what is known as the *fall line*—the most direct route between the point where you are at any given moment and the bottom of the hill.

(2) Centrifugal force is the force throwing us to the outside of the turn. The faster and tighter the turn, the greater the centrifugal force; the slower and wider the turn, the smaller the centrifugal force.

(3) Friction between the skis' edges and the snow enables us to manage gravity and centrifugal force. As long as the skis are moving straight ahead, friction is minimal. When skis are at an angle to the line of travel, friction increases.

The reason we slow down and eventually come to a stop when we ski directly *across* the hill is that the friction generated by the bite of the edges resists the pull of gravity.

15 From the Edges Up

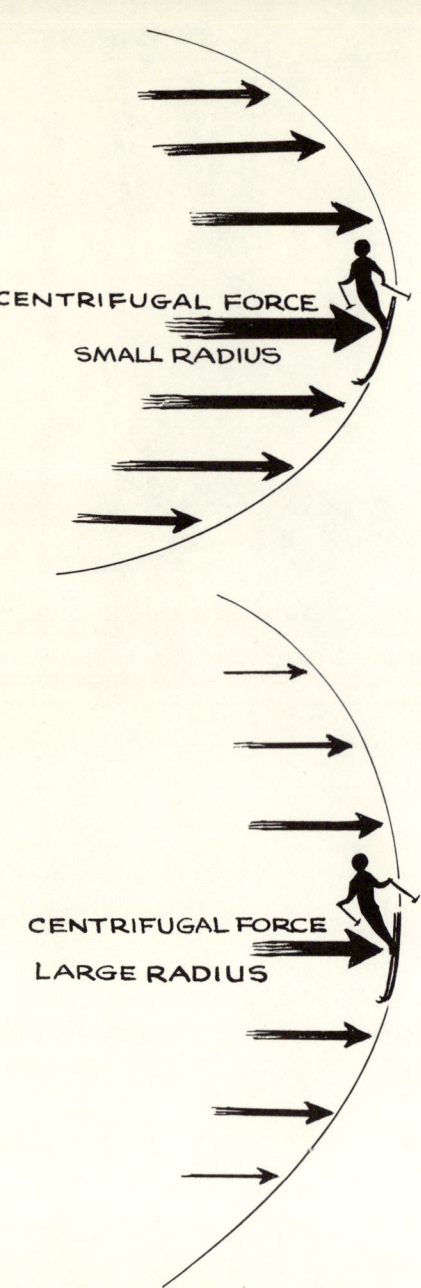

Centrifugal force is the force you feel trying to throw you to the outside of the turn. The faster and tighter the turn (top), the greater the centrifugal force. Slowing down or increasing the arc of the turn reduces the effects of centrifugal force (bottom).

Similarly, friction prevents the skis from skidding out of a turn when subjected to centrifugal force provided the skis are edged sufficiently.

For all practical purposes, the edges control the skis through friction. Skiing is the art of manipulating the edges.

Edging: The Skill and the Tools

"Skiing is edging," a technique guru once said. Although he was oversimplifying, he was not far wrong. Virtually everything we do in skiing is for the purpose of bringing the edges into play or a consequence of the interaction between the edges and the snow. For these reasons, all of the elements involved in edge control deserve the most careful scrutiny.

Crucial though it is, there is nothing mysterious about edge control. Basically, all that it requires is appropriate changes in the angle of the skis to the snow and sufficient pressure on the skis to make the edges bite. In practice it is much more subtle. Every situation in skiing has slightly different edging requirements. There is no mechanical way to define them all. You have to develop a feel for the edges as they bite into the snow and train yourself to make adjustments until you get the response you want.

The Ski Better Book

When the skis are pointed straight downhill and are flat on the snow, they're virtually frictionless. When they're at an angle to the fall line and on edge, friction increases—more if the skis are skidding than when they're carving, which is why the snowplow slows you down, even when you're going straight down the hill. In the latter case, the friction of one ski opposes the other, resulting in heavy braking. When the skis are across the hill in a traverse, friction is at a maximum and you'll eventually come to a stop if you run out of momentum.

Sideslipping to Edge Control

The best way to demonstrate the range of control the edges provide and to develop your feel for the edges is by practicing the **sideslipping** exercises illustrated.

Start by standing at the top of the hill with the skis directly across the fall line —directly across the hill. Getting yourself into that position already gives you a clue to what's involved. Your skis will slip to the side—sideslip—unless they are sufficiently on edge to prevent them from doing so. Sideslipping is the **controlled** sideways motion of the skis and this control is achieved by varying the angle of the edges to the snow.

Unless you're on a fairly steep pitch, you'll probably experience some difficulty in making the skis sideslip when starting from a stationary position: Even though you've **released** the edges— reduced the angle the edges make with the snow—the skis won't slide because the friction of the stationary ski directly across the line of intended travel is greater than the force of gravity. Releasing the edges more may get the skis started, but don't overdo it; if you allow the edges on the downhill side of the skis to catch, you'll tumble. Another frequent problem is that one ski will slip more readily than the other. Equipment may be the cause, but usually it's due to not releasing the edges evenly on both skis or to carrying too much weight on the uphill ski.

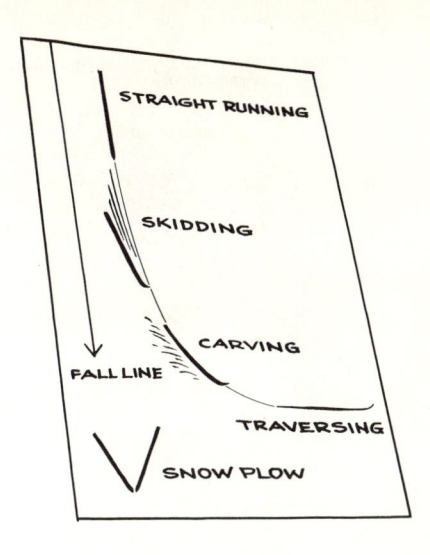

Sideslipping is actually easier and more realistic if you do it while **traversing**—skiing across the hill—since moving skis slip more readily and don't require as steep a pitch to start slipping. For this exercise and the one to follow pick a hill with a long, easy run-out so that if something does go haywire, you'll have a way to slow down.

Begin by skiing straight across the slope with the skis just sufficiently on edge to prevent them from slipping (you may have to roll your knees slightly into

17 From the Edges Up

To prevent the skis from sliding when they're facing across the hill, keep them on edge by rolling the knees into the hill (a). To make a controlled sideslip, release the edges by rolling the knees away from the hill (b) and then adjust the edge angle to govern the speed of descent (c). To stop the slide, increase the edge angle sharply (d).

---

the hill to accomplish this). To start slipping, gradually roll the knees away from the hill to release the bite of the edges. As the skis start to slip sideways, one of three things will happen:

(1) The skis will continue pointing directly across the fall line while simultaneously slipping forward and sideways, resulting in a diagonal skid across the hill.

(2) The tips will slide downhill faster than the tails.

(3) The tails will slide downhill faster than the tips.

You can control what the skis do, but as you will find in most skiing situations, there is more than one way to get the job done. In this particular situation, it depends on how much you release the edges and where the pressure is on the skis.

When you release the edges just slightly, the skis will slip sideways slowly because friction remains relatively high. If you lean forward, the pressure, and therefore the friction, will increase at the tip and decrease at the tails resulting in situation A; the tails will slide downhill faster than the tips. If you do nothing about this motion of the skis, they will turn uphill and you will come to a stop.

The Ski Better Book 18

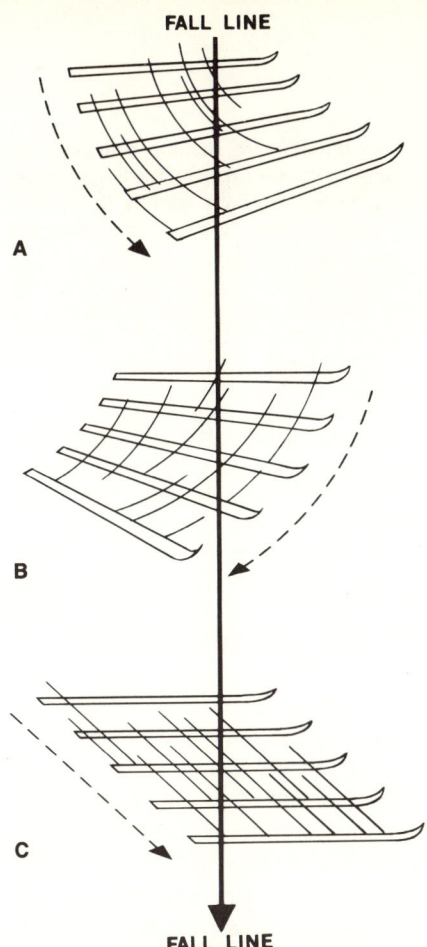

a

b

c

Conversely, if you lean back with the edges just slightly released, the skis will turn into the fall line as in B.

When you stand evenly on your skis, applying neither backward nor forward pressure, the skis will travel diagonally across the hill as in C.

Take care when sideslipping on gentle slopes and in loose snow, where it becomes easy to overdo the edge release and trip yourself by catching the downhill edge (b and c).

Complete Reversal

As you release the edges more, the results are the **complete reverse** of those with the edges slightly released.

With friction almost as low as it can get with the skis directly across the fall line, the effects of gravity overwhelm whatever friction remains. As a result, when you lean forward and put pressure on the tips of the skis, the tips will go downhill faster than the tails as in B. When you put pressure on the tails, they go downhill faster than the tips as in A.

19   From the Edges Up

Once the skis are slipping sideways, increasing the pressure on the backs of the skis by leaning back slightly (a) causes the tails to slide downhill faster than the tips. Returning to the neutral position checks this tails-first slide (c). Increasing the pressure on the fronts of the skis by leaning forward makes the tips slide downhill faster than the tails (d–f). The tips-first slide is checked by again returning to the neutral position (g). This exercise, sometimes called the falling leaf, can be used to work your way around and between obstacles that you may not want to tackle head-on.

Precise Control

One of the immediate advantages that sideslipping and the edging skills it involves give you is precise control over your skis and the ability to determine their rate of descent. Before you tackle more difficult terrain, you should be able to slip the skis in any direction and make any corrections necessary to get to the point on the slope where you intended to go. This provides you with an important safety valve. If you should find yourself on a pitch you are not sure you can handle safely, you can traverse-sideslip across it until you get to a point where you can turn easily, or you can sideslip straight down until you are back on terrain with which you are comfortable.

It has probably occurred to you by now that sideslipping, or rather the control you have over edge angle and the pressure on the skis, is the basis for turning the skis. You can now make the skis turn uphill and come to a stop by letting the tails slide faster than the tips (this is called an uphill christie). You can

The Ski Better Book   20

also turn the skis downhill by letting the tips slide faster than the tails. The catch is that as the skis approach the fall line, they will no longer slip to the side. Since the skis are now pointed almost straight downhill, friction in the direction they are going has become low. They will keep going that way unless you can somehow keep them turning.

Edge Change

If you keep riding the same set of edges that you used at the beginning of the sideslip, you will not get a true change of direction. All you can do—short of going straight downhill—is go across the slope in the direction you were originally going in a series of slips. Making a complete turn requires a change from the edges you are using to the opposite edges. This is called edge change and

If, in turning out of the fall line (a), you release the edges and lean back (b), the tails of the skis will slide downhill (c), and the skis will turn uphill (d) and bring you to a stop. This is called an uphill or stop christie and it's an important safety maneuver. The sharpness of the uphill turn depends on how much the edges are released and the amount of backward lean.

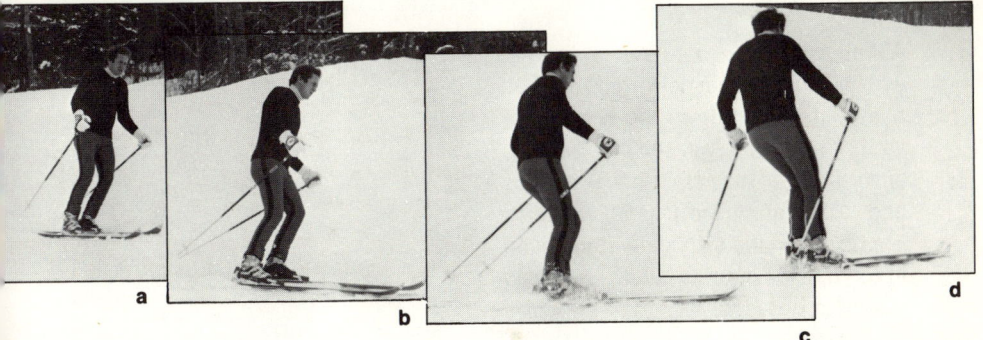

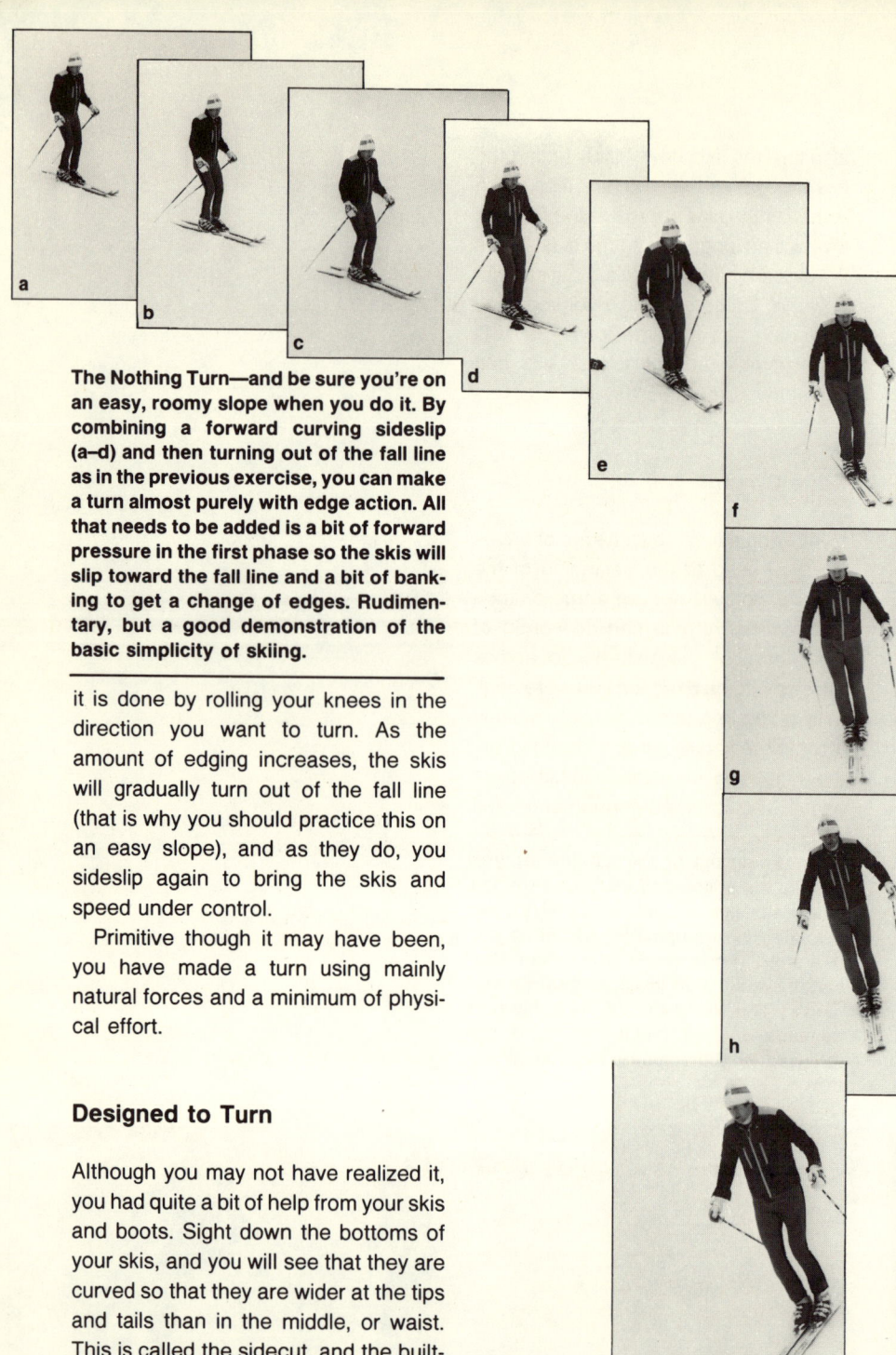

The Nothing Turn—and be sure you're on an easy, roomy slope when you do it. By combining a forward curving sideslip (a–d) and then turning out of the fall line as in the previous exercise, you can make a turn almost purely with edge action. All that needs to be added is a bit of forward pressure in the first phase so the skis will slip toward the fall line and a bit of banking to get a change of edges. Rudimentary, but a good demonstration of the basic simplicity of skiing.

it is done by rolling your knees in the direction you want to turn. As the amount of edging increases, the skis will gradually turn out of the fall line (that is why you should practice this on an easy slope), and as they do, you sideslip again to bring the skis and speed under control.

Primitive though it may have been, you have made a turn using mainly natural forces and a minimum of physical effort.

Designed to Turn

Although you may not have realized it, you had quite a bit of help from your skis and boots. Sight down the bottoms of your skis, and you will see that they are curved so that they are wider at the tips and tails than in the middle, or waist. This is called the sidecut, and the built-in curve helps the skis to turn when you put them on edge.

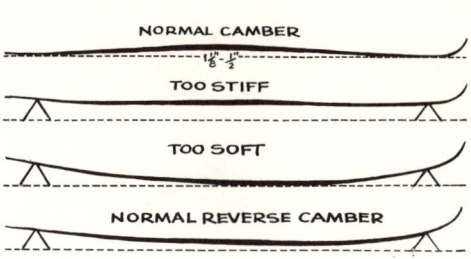

Sidecut is a subtle quality and difficult to judge by casual inspection. It is exaggerated here for purposes of illustration only. The sidecut helps to make the ski turn when the ski is put on edge.

The ability of the ski to flex from camber to various degrees of reverse camber enhances the skis' turning ability.

Ski boots, the vital tools in the transmission of side-to-side and forward-backward leg motions to the skis.

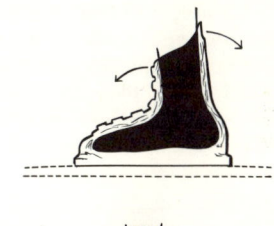

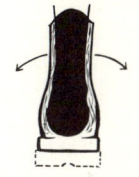

You will also notice that the skis are not flat, but are built convexly, like a leaf spring. This feature is called **camber** and, when your weight is on the skis, it flattens out. When the skis are put on edge, the skis bend even more, into **reverse camber.** This further emphasizes their tendency to turn.

The more skis are on edge, the more they can bend into reverse camber because the narrower waist can bend more than the tails or tips before making firm snow contact.

In essence, the more we can edge our skis, the more reverse camber we get, and the sharper we can make our turns.

Edging and shifting the center of pressure on the skis would be extremely difficult were it not for the boots. The boots don't merely supply ankle support but, being almost totally rigid laterally, translate the slightest side-to-side leg movement into a change in edge angle. Although they are more flexible in the fore-aft direction, the boots also transmit forward and backward movement of the legs.

23 From the Edges Up

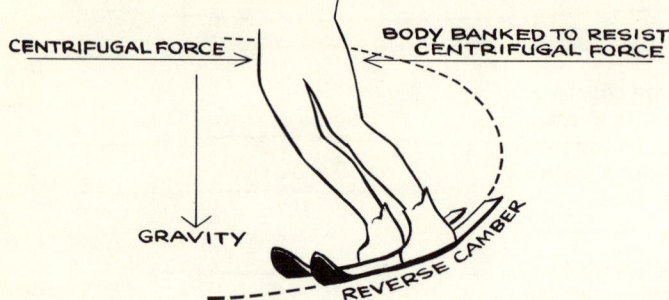

Both gravity and centrifugal force act on the skier in a turn. Banking counteracts centrifugal force and creates a force that exerts a direct downward pressure on the skis and bends them into reverse camber—providing the skis are edged enough to prevent them from slipping to the side.

Back to Balance

Recall that centrifugal force is the force that throws us to the outside of a turn. By proper body positioning, this force can be utilized to put pressure on the skis, bending them into reverse camber to help us make the skis turn. Consequently, balance and body positioning are not merely means of staying upright but are vital ingredients to make the skis function. We will cover this topic in the next chapter, but let us stay with edging skills a little longer.

It is quite apparent that drifting through the turn by sideslipping and changing edges in the fall line is not fast or precise enough for most ski conditions. You would be out of control even before you reached the fall line. So in practical skiing, you do not wait until the skis are almost in the fall line before you change edges, but rather change edges at the very beginning of the turn, usually with some kind of a boost to get the turn started, which is discussed in detail in Chapter 5, "Turn Initiation." Making the edge change at the beginning of the turn makes possible a much faster, more tightly controlled turn and takes maximum advantage of the built-in turning capabilities of the skis, which are greatly enhanced because a rapid change of direction increases centrifugal force and reverse camber with it.

Carve, Don't Skid

Although sideslipping exercises are excellent vehicles for mastering the elements of edge control, better skiers make every effort to **minimize skidding** in turns. Skidding skis are essentially the same as skidding cars—out of control. At lower speeds this is not especially critical, but it becomes a serious drawback in advanced skiing. If you are skidding, the edges cannot do their work; precise, fast turning becomes extremely difficult; and it takes a lot of useless body motion and energy to get the skis to do their job.

The Ski Better Book 24

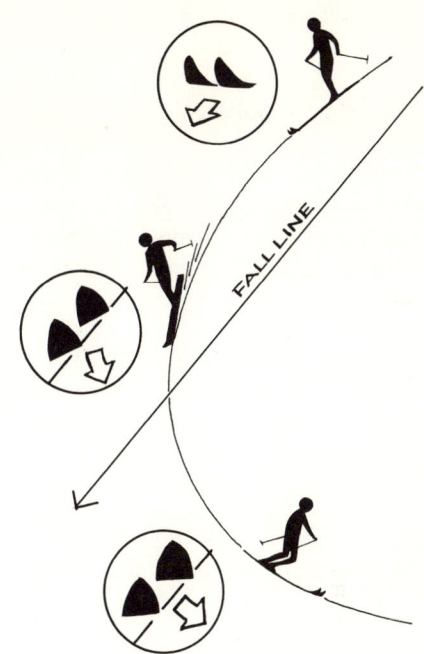

Edging is not a mechanical either/or type of motion. You must learn to sense how much edging is required for the radius of the turn you want to make and adjust the edging accordingly. As the skis accelerate going through the fall line, edge angle has to be increased to maintain the carving action and to prevent the skis from skidding.

I mention this point because I want to stress that edge control is a dynamic activity requiring constant adjustment of edge angle and pressure throughout the turn. The pitch of the slope is constantly changing, sometimes drastically. Although an edge change can be made very quickly, it is not instantaneous; at the same time, the skis are heading for the fall line and are subject to the effects of increasing acceleration and centrifugal force.

If you want to maintain a turn of a given radius, you have to constantly, but subtly, increase edge angle until you are well out of the fall line and the skis have stopped accelerating. In tight turns, where centrifugal force is high, too much forward pressure may cause the tails to skid despite extreme edging and you will have to reduce this pressure, even resort to back pressure, to prevent it.

You cannot just make a move and expect something to happen. You have to be in constant motion, not merely reacting to the situation, but anticipating it.

Points of Emphasis

Because edging is so crucial to skiing, and because I will be making constant references to it throughout the rest of the book, I will sum up the key points for ready reference:

(1) Skis are controlled by combining and varying the effects of gravity and centrifugal force with friction and pressure.

(2) Skis are designed to be sensitive to changes in friction and pressure.

(3) The amount of friction at the edges is determined by the angle of the edges to the snow and pressure on the skis.

(4) A shift in pressure toward the tip or tail makes the skis change direction as long as they are on edge.

(5) You suffer at least partial loss of control if there is no pressure on the skis since it makes the skis frictionless for all practical purposes.

(6) To vary pressure and friction requires a firm linkage between you and your skis; in other words, your boots must be stiff enough to convert the sideways motion of your legs into changes of edge angle and their forward-backward motions into pressure on the tips and tails.

Three
Balance: The Means to an End

We all know how to balance. Standing in a swaying bus, we spread our feet. Walking on a narrow beam, we stretch our arms out to the sides. Coming around a corner on a bicycle, we lean to the inside of the turn (bank). Standing on one leg, we shift our body slightly so that our weight is centered on the leg we are standing on. We do this unconsciously. When we feel the balance shift, we compensate. We **consciously** try to maintain our balance only in **extreme** situations.

The problem with balancing on skis is that, to most inexperienced skiers, skiing **is** an extreme situation. The skis are slippery, and the terrain is constantly changing in pitch and configuration. The strange technical demands of skiing seem to restrict freedom of movement. Conceded, skiing is a bit more acrobatic than most other sports. But balancing on skis becomes relatively simple if you break it down into its component parts, then work on educating your sense of balance.

Find Your Groove

Basic to balance is a stable, natural, comfortable stance with your weight squarely over the skis. Your feet should be about under your hips, about four to eight inches apart. Ankles, knees, and waist should be slightly flexed so that you can absorb the shocks of the terrain, like an accordion. The hands should be held somewhat ahead and to the sides of the body just above waist level.

This stance—a position of athletic readiness found in many sports—is not

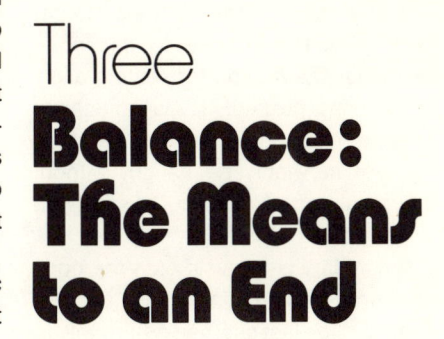

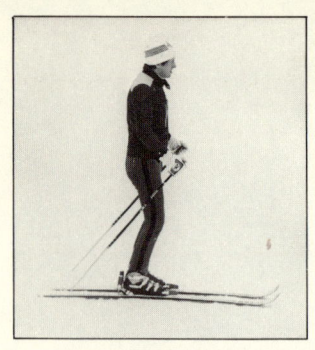

The basic stance is just that. Think of it as the point where you have maximum freedom of movement. Note especially the bend at the knees. If you straighten them, you have, in effect, blocked your shock absorbers.

---

a textbook pose. You will have to experiment to find out what is most comfortable for you. Every person is slightly different, and you will need to try various combinations to find the groove that gives you maximum stability without interfering with your ability to maneuver.

Don't strike a pose; be yourself. If you have difficulty with the feet at hip width, spread your feet a bit more. Try spreading your arms farther apart or lowering your center of gravity, or use your poles.

The basic stance is not a frozen body position once the skis are in motion. You should consider it merely as a reference point where you have the widest latitude in moving up and down, backward and forward, and from side to side. It is merely common sense to get back somewhere close to this point whenever the reason for shifting away from it has passed. If you constantly operate at the outer fringes of balance, you will inevitably be caught without that small reserve that could save you from a fall.

A corollary is to avoid extreme body positions and motions. As demonstrated in the last chapter, nature will do a large portion of the work if you allow it to. Unless the terrain is extreme or you are stunting, you do not need wild upper-body gyrations. If you have to resort to them, there is something lacking in your basic skills, or the equipment (see Chapter 4) you are using is not suitable to your needs.

Improving Balance

As noted in the last chapter, you must learn to balance on skis before you get on the hill. One of the best, safest exercises that familiarizes you with both balance and edge control is skating on the flat, which emphasizes the dynamic relationship between the two, good timing, and the need for body mobility to maintain balance.

On-the-hill work on balance starts with straight running down the fall line of an easy slope. You're probably familiar with this simple exercise from your very first lesson, but it's also an excellent means for further sharpening your kinesthetic senses as you improve. Start out in a basic stance, but don't freeze into that position. Keep your knees loose to absorb the shock of the bumps and uneven terrain; demonstrate to yourself how much you can move forward and backward and to the sides without losing your balance; and feel the increase of stability as you

The Ski Better Book   28

Skating on skis is just like skating with ice skates. Note, however, that you also have poles. Before starting, make sure they're well off the ground so that they don't get tangled in the tails of your skis. In the beginning use small steps and work up to more aggressive skating as you gain proficiency. Pick up the right ski, angle it away from the left, and at the same time face the direction you intend to go (a). Meanwhile put the left ski on its inside edge and push off (b). As the thrust from the push is at its maximum, place the right ski on the snow and glide (d) and bring the left ski back under you, angling it just as you did the right ski in (a). Now push off the right ski for the next step (e–f) and keep it up.

---

widen your stance, lower your center of gravity, and spread your arms to the sides.

You will find that side-to-side balance is more difficult to maintain than fore-aft balance, particularly in the earlier stages. In straight running, you're most stable when your body weight is equally suspended between both legs and with both knees equally flexed, but when skiing across the hill in a traverse or in a turn, you have to increase the bend in your uphill knee to achieve this effect.

To avoid having to bend the knee excessively on steeper slopes, the uphill hip, leg, and ski are advanced slightly and, for stability's sake, slightly more weight is carried on the downhill ski. This latter adjustment is crucial to prevent teetering precariously on the uphill ski as the slope steepens—and on the inside ski when turning. Psychologically, this shifting of the weight to the downhill and outside ski is one of the sport's toughest hurdles. Just as most of us tend to shy away from looking over the side of tall buildings, so

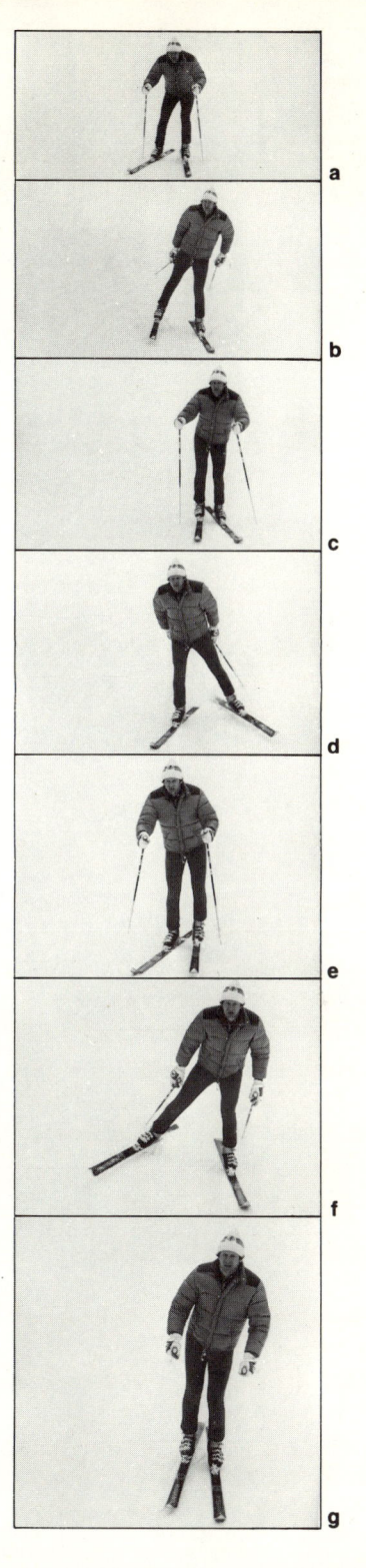

29   Balance: The Means to an End

Scooter skating is a simplified form of two-step skating. Instead of skating from leg to leg, angle the left ski away from the right, put it on its inside edge, and push off (a). Glide on the right leg and bring the left leg back under you, still angled (b). Repeat the process for a distance and then change legs, pushing off with the right.

most of us tend to duck away from what seems to be leaning out over the hill. The only way to overcome this tendency is to *feel* the stability that comes from having your weight properly placed over the skis.

Functional Balance

Your initial concern in balancing will be to stay upright, but good balance is not merely a matter of not falling, but rather of positioning the body so the skis can do their job.

In the previous chapter, particularly in the section on sideslipping, you saw how the skis responded to changes in edge angle and in the distribution of pressure on the skis. In a given turn, the need for these changes depends on the terrain, and it is the position of the skis in relation to the slope that determines what we have to do to stay in balance. Balance—that is, just staying on your feet and not falling—doesn't help much unless you stand properly on your skis so they can function.

This is perhaps easier to demonstrate than to define, but over-simplifying a bit, it is basically standing on the skis in such a way that you can generate the friction necessary to control the skis. This can only be done if your weight is over the skis, or more specifically still, over the edges so that they can bite into the snow.

The necessity for balancing to keep your weight over the skis is already apparent in straight running where, if you lean back beyond a certain point, the pressure, instead of being above the skis, comes from behind and shoves the skis out from under you.

Modern boots with higher backs, which convert backward lean into downward pressure on the skis, have reduced this particular difficulty to some extent, but haven't completely eliminated it, particularly on steeper slopes. You can cure this problem by making it a habit in all normal skiing to lean forward from the ankles until you feel your shins pressing lightly on the fronts of your boots.

The need for functional balance becomes even more apparent when you are traversing and turning. As you get on steeper slopes, you'll notice that you have to make a much more positive effort to edge the skis to keep them from slipping or skidding. At first you can get the desired amount of edging by rolling up your ankles, but beyond a certain point this is no longer enough: You have to push your knees into the hill. This motion shifts your weight from directly over your skis to their uphill side and actually decreases the amount of edge bite. To counteract this you must make a compensatory balancing movement of the upper body in a downhill direction so that your weight again is bearing directly down on your edges. This characteristic movement of the upper body leaning away from the hill is called **angulation,** and the steeper the hill and the more severe the turn, the more angulation is required.

Nature Assists

In changing edges at the start of a turn, legs and body are banked toward the inside of the turn to achieve the necessary change of edge angle. This seems to be a rather drastic movement of the hips to the inside of the turn. However, providing it is not overdone, nature provides an assist here in the form of centrifugal force, which not only counters the tendency for the hips to drop toward the inside of the turn but also has the added benefit of putting extra pressure on the edges.

It is possible, if the turn is fast and tight, for the edge angle in banking to become so great that further banking no longer puts adequate down-pressure on the skis. To prevent this, legs are maintained at the proper edge angle, but the upper body is angulated toward the outside of the turn and maintains the combined thrust of the bank and centrifugal force straight down on the edges.

You can further increase angulation by twisting your upper body so that it faces the outside of the turn. This moves the hip out of the way so that you can angle your upper body even more to the outside of the turn.

A much more solid position on skis results if the ski on the outside of the turn carries somewhat more of the weight than the inside ski as noted on page 29. At the start of a turn, this calls for a shift of weight to the outside ski, but once the ski starts to turn, centrifugal force will keep the pressure on it, providing you do not frustrate nature by stiffening or straightening out the inside leg.

For good balance, more of your weight must be on the downhill ski when you're traversing and on the outside ski when you're turning. As long as the slope is gentle or the turns long-radiused and slow, all that's needed to transfer the extra weight is to drop your hip slightly (a). As the slope gets steeper and the turns faster and tighter and you have to roll your knees and hips into the hill to maintain the required edging, you have to make an equally emphatic compensatory movement to keep the weight where it belongs. This is done by bending the upper body sideways at the waist (b) and is called angulation. In racing-type turns (c), where bank angle is large, sideways bending at the waist is no longer enough. In that situation, the hip is twisted toward the outside of the turn and the body is bent forward at the waist. This shifts weight to the outside of the ski, which is where you want it.

Although balancing has been separated here for the purposes of instruction, the sooner you meld **balance** with **edging** skills, the more rapidly you will progress. They are the rock-bottom fundamentals involved in every skiing maneuver. Become proficient in both, and your battle to master skiing is more than half won.

The Ski Better Book

You probably started off on rented equipment and sensed that it was not 100-percent satisfactory, even though you could not pinpoint whether it was you or the equipment that was the problem. Somewhere along the line you have already been urged to get your own boots, skis, bindings, and poles and you have tentatively explored the possibility. No doubt you have been thoroughly confused by all the different models and shocked by the prices they charge for all this stuff.

You can get a better perspective on the problem if you start out by thinking of equipment in terms of our first principle: *get all the mileage you can.*

For instance, if you have constant difficulties in finding rental boots that fit, you are going to have trouble accumulating maximum mileage, either because you have to spend so much time finding a suitable pair or because you will not be able to go all out when the boots hurt. Similarly, if you are exceptionally heavy or light, there may be problems in finding a suitable pair of skis, as most rental shops are stocked for skiers who conform more closely to the norm. Without proper skis, you will not only fall more, which wastes a lot of time, but you will have a hard time cultivating the smoothness and rhythm that are the hallmarks of the good skier.

Experience Is the Best Guide

As for what to buy from among hundreds of models of skis, boots, bindings, and poles from over sixty major brand names, your *experience* reinforced by your *awareness* of the rela-

Four
Equipment

tionship between equipment and basic skiing skills are your best guides. Generally, the characteristics of the equipment determine how you will execute the basic skills.

For instance, if you are too light for the skis, it will be difficult for you to flatten them against the snow and, consequently, to sideslip smoothly. For this particular reason, avoid becoming overawed by brands and models used by ski instructors, racers, and local hot shots. Their equipment is not necessarily bad for you, but difficult as it may be sometimes, you should make every effort to make sure it is suitable for your specific needs.

Season Rentals

Short of buying, the best approach to equipment is to rent or lease for the season. You can have yourself fitted out just as if you were buying, and the boots and skis are assigned to you so that you do not have to go through the fitting procedure every time you take the gear out. Unfortunately, shops with rental arrangements of this type are few and far between.

Although there are all kinds of pressures on the new skier to shoot the works, resist especially the lure of "that old pair of boards" your friend has in his closet and the packages that ski shops and sporting goods stores put together to entice you to buy more than you actually need. Too often, one or more items in these packages will be out-dated, odd-sized, and of poor quality. Even if you plan to buy your own equipment as soon as possible, make it a practice to shop for one item at a time. It is hard enough to keep straight all the information that will be shot at you about boots without having to think about skis, bindings, and poles.

Buy equipment only as you need it. A visit to a ski shop will make you realize there are no hard and fast rules to guide you in selecting equipment. Finding what is right for you is a matter of trial and error. The more inexperienced you are the greater your chance for error.

If you buy too soon, you may outgrow your equipment before getting your money's worth out of it. It is better to hold off until you have a better idea of how far you are likely to go and how fast you are likely to get there. You will not only have a better estimate of what *your* needs are, but, by spending some time talking with other skiers first and comparing their skill and weight with yours, you will also learn what brands and models are likely to satisfy you. Besides, by waiting until later in the season you often can get substantial discounts at end-of-sea-

There's such a vast assortment of skis, boots, and other ski equipment that you'll have difficulty in making a wise choice until you've built up some experience with various brands and models.

son clearance sales, which usually start around the end of January.

Start with Boots

More than likely, the first equipment you will buy are boots. You need not be an expert to see why; your feet give you the message.

Rental boots rarely fit well. Without proper fit, no boots can deliver the performance you expect from them.

Boots have changed drastically in the last decade, and in the process they have revolutionized the sport. Unfortunately, those who sell boots have not thoroughly understood this. There is still a strong tendency to steer inexperienced skiers away from models that promise "performance," meaning boots that enable you to put pressure on the skis by pressing forward *and* backward with the legs. If you tell the boot salesman that you are just getting into skiing, he will invariably try to sell you a model that will do little more than connect you to your skis and keep your feet warm.

Occasionally, you may encounter a salesman who recognizes no middle ground and immediately wants you to jump into the hottest boot in the shop, but fortunately they are rare. More frequently, you will run across the bootman who learned his business in the leather boot era and cannot get over the fact that modern plastic boots do not "break in." He will make light of pressure points and imperfect fit and assure you they will go away. It is your job to tell him that you know they won't. Make him dig around for a better-fitting pair. With good boots at eighty dollars and up, there is no excuse for not providing a good fit.

Good fit is essential for comfort but it is also essential for proper function. Boots can be compared to an automobile transmission, transmitting the movements of the legs to the skis. If they are loose, the clutch slips, and if too tight, the gears will bind. The feeling you are seeking when trying on boots is frequently described as snug, but has been more accurately described by a skiing podiatrist as "all-around containment."

The boot should grip the foot, ankle, heel and lower leg firmly (except for the toes, which should be free to wiggle). Yet, it must not be so tight that it cuts off circulation.

In terms of function, boots for all skiers are almost totally rigid laterally so that they can transmit the slightest side-

Even a well-equipped rental shop may have problems in providing you with well-fitting boots. Since they're critically important for both comfort and performance, boots are usually the first item on the skier's shopping list.

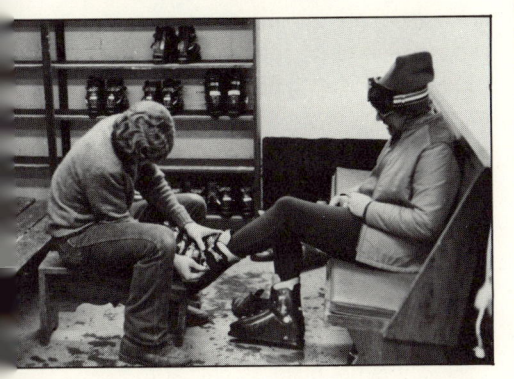

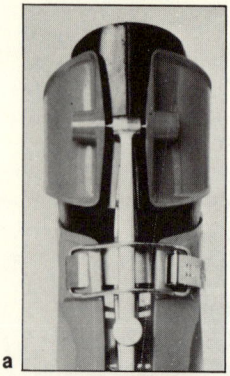

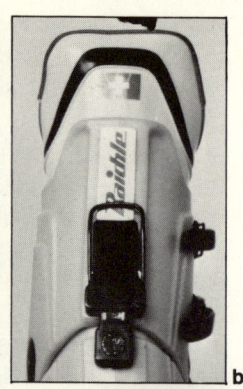

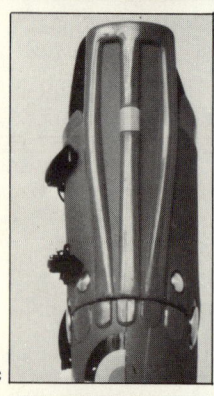

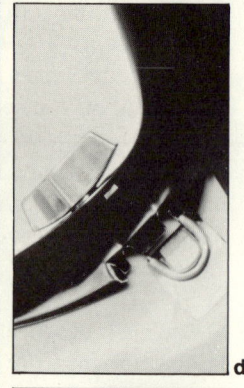

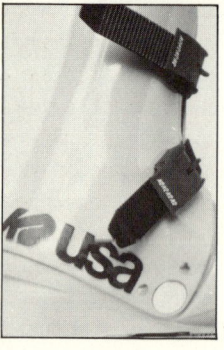

Special features—such as the calf-width and canting adjustment (a), the forward lean adjustment (b), the flex button (c) that can be taken out to make the back more flexible, and unusual buckle arrangements (d–f)—may solve some individual adjustment problems, but boots with these features should be bought only after you're sure you have a proper fit.

to-side movement of the legs into a change of edge angle and provide strong ankle support when the skis are being edged hard. However, some skiers find the mechanical advantage of their legs too great to make subtle edge adjustments, so they prefer a little bit of lateral freedom in the boot to make these adjustments with ankle movements. This is a purely personal preference and, by loosening the top buckles in the boots a notch, you can determine if you like this feeling.

Up to a point, the higher the boots, the more effectively you can transform the leverage of the leg into pressure on the skis and the stiffer the boots in the fore-aft direction, the more efficient the transformation. Higher, stiffer boots have the capability of producing almost instant response at the skis. This is a plus for the strong, advanced skier, but a handicap for the inexperienced skier whose lack of smoothness and precision will be instantly and faithfully reproduced at the skis.

On the basis of comfort and cost alone, you should buy boots no higher and stiffer than necessary. The stiffer and higher the boots, the more difficult they are to fit. And the more difficult to fit, the more expensive they are likely to be.

Height is not quite as critical to performance as stiffness. Inasmuch as it increases leverage and distributes the pressure against the shin over a wider area, it is an advantage for most skiers to have high boots. However, when the boot back—always higher to provide support in leaning backward—reaches mid-calf height, a point of diminishing returns sets in, particularly in softer boots, and there is no point in buying height for height's sake except to look like a hot skier.

How do you know when the boot is right? Stiffness is to some extent a personal matter, but if you can push your knee forward so it is directly over the toe without straining, the boot is about right for you. You should feel sharply increasing resistance beyond this point if you are an advanced skier, a more gradual increase in resistance if you are still in the novice-intermediate ranks.

Boot selection is easier if you have taken careful note of the problems you

---

The vast majority of boots currently on the market use five buckles. However, the number can vary from one to six. Boots with fewer buckles are more convenient to put on, but may not provide fine enough fit adjustment if your feet are oddly shaped or swell or shrink noticeably during the day.

Height of the outer shell as such is not an indication of the boot's performance capabilities. Although both appear to be about the same, the boot on the left (a) is for good recreational skiers while the one on the right (b) is for the serious competitor. Note that the shell of the boot on the right—not the inner boot that sticks up above it—is actually somewhat higher than that of the left boot. You'd have to try both boots to determine the difference between them.

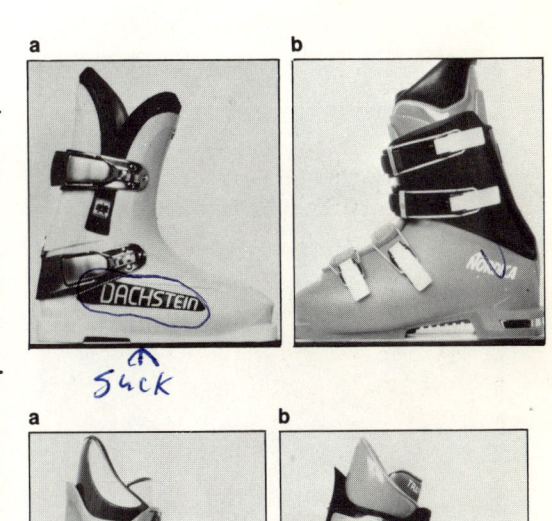

37 Equipment

encountered with rental boots. You will know if your new boots measure up simply by comparison. One of the best tests is to spend some time simulating ski maneuvers, or better still, doing them on a ski exerciser. This will bring out any problems you might not have noticed while you were trying them on.

If you experience minor pressure points—usually at the ball of the foot or the ankle bones—it does not mean the boot is no good. The ski shop has special equipment to remove these before you leave the store.

Though boots seem to fit, you may still encounter problems on the slopes. Don't be alarmed. You may have buckled up too tight at the beginning of the day. Your feet and legs may not be properly conditioned. You may have a wrinkle in your sock, or the boots simply need further tuning. The best procedure is to take it easy when you first use new boots. Do not force the issue if you encounter severe pain or feel blisters coming on. It is better to ski in rental boots than to ski in agony.

Skis

Rental skis are not always the greatest. As the season goes along, they suffer increasingly from wear and tear. It is

---

The variety of brands and models in rental shops is usually quite limited. However, most shops stock a few samples—demos—of the skis they sell. When you are seriously thinking of buying skis, try some of these demos to see if they meet your needs. Also (top), take advantage of the manufacturers' demo programs whenever their vans visit your area.

The Ski Better Book 38

hard to find a set with sharp edges, smooth bottoms, and bindings that at least look confidence-inspiring. It is usually at this point that you begin to think about buying skis and bindings (one is no use without the other) of your own.

Picking a pair of skis is both simple and complicated. It is simple because once you get over the hundred-dollar level you cannot go too far wrong. It is complicated because the number of models has proliferated beyond the comprehension of all but a few experts.

The easiest, though not always the best, way out of this dilemma is to find a ski shop that shows some understanding of your problem and let the salesman make the choice for you. If that is going to be your approach, it will help the salesman greatly if he knows the lengths, models, and brands you have been using, how quickly you were able to progress from one length to the next, how good a skier you are now and the kind of skiing—recreational, freestyle, or racing—you are interested in, where and how often you ski, and how

---

Although there are hundreds of models available, all except a handful of specialty skis fall into one of six categories: racing skis (a), which come in downhill, slalom, and giant slalom versions; full-length recreational skis (b) that are sized and flexed to give optimum performance when the ski is six to ten inches longer than the skier is tall; freestyle skis (c) for stunts and very fast turning; high-performance short skis (d), which are usually shorter, somewhat wider versions of racing or other high-performance skis from a given manufacturer; recreational short skis (e) for intermediate and casual skiers; and learning or GLM skis (f) for beginners and ski-school use.

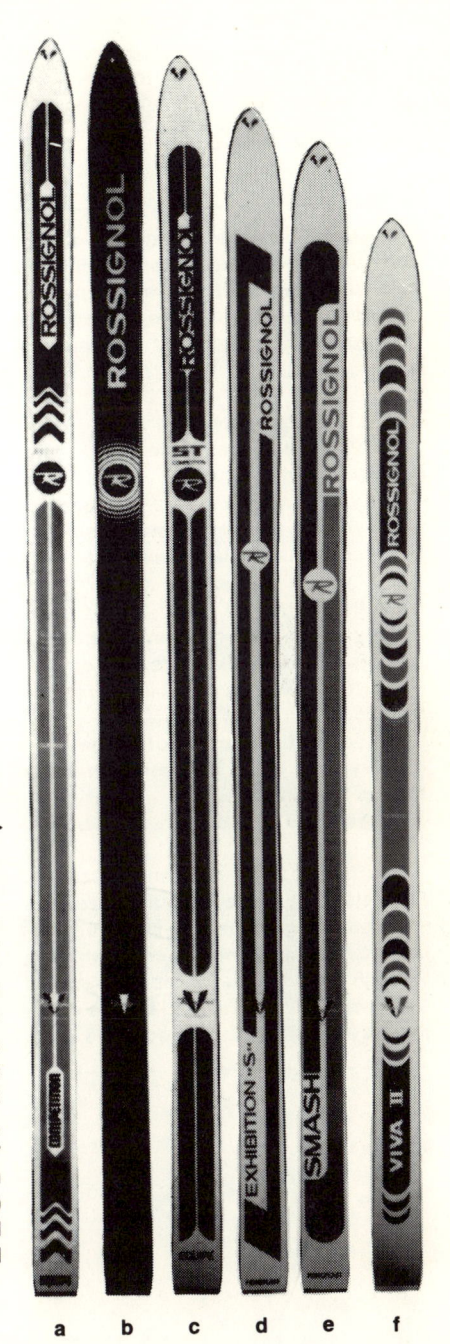

39 Equipment

	Inexperienced Skier*		Experienced Skiers				Racers	
Your Weight	Interm.	Advanced	Aspiring Expert	Expert	Aggressive Freestyle	Slalom	Giant Slalom	Down-Hill
100 to 115 lbs.	150	160	165	175	160	185	195	200
115 to 130 lbs.	155	165	170	180	165	190	200	205
130 to 145 lbs.	160	170	175	185	170	195	205	210
145 to 160 lbs.	165	175	180	190	175	200	207	215
160 to 175 lbs.	170	180	185	203	180	205	210	220
175 to 190 lbs.	175	185	190	205	185	207	212	220
190 lbs. or more	180	190	195	210	190	208	215	220

* BEGINNERS SHOULD RENT SKIS

This sizing chart based on your weight and ability gives you a starting point to help you determine the correct length of skis for you. After you've picked your size from the chart, adjust the figure as follows.

Add five centimeters
—if you weigh in at close to the upper limit indicated,
—if you're athletic and a fast learner,
—if you are more interested in stability at speed than maneuverability in turning,
—if you're especially tall for your weight,
—if you use stiff, non-hinging boots.

Subtract five centimeters
—if your weight is at the lower limit indicated,
—if you're timid or out of shape,
—if you're more interested in quick turning than in speed,
—if you use soft, easy-hinging boots.

Use the net figure counting all factors. For instance, you may be athletic and use stiff, non-hinging boots—plus 10 cm—but are especially interested in wiggling through tight moguls—minus 5 cm. In that case, your skis should be five centimeters longer than indicated in the table.

much you are willing to pay for skis and bindings **combined.** One of the signs of a good salesman is how interested he is in your particular problems and how thoroughly he explores your needs before making his recommendation.

Unfortunately, first-rate ski salesmen are scarce and, since they are not too sure what all the skis in their racks will really do, there is the strong tendency to play it safe. The tendency is to sell you skis that will probably be adequate for the present, but will not be up to the performance you will demand a year later. That is why I have suggested that you hold off buying skis until you have accumulated some experience with skis and have some basis for judgment.

As the itch to buy grows stronger, start paying close attention to the ski test reports in major ski publications. Although these reports are sparse in hard, specific information, they do provide enough character and performance information either to serve as a check on your ski shop's recommendation or, if you are doing your own selecting, to let you zero in on skis that deserve your serious consideration.

Next, take a careful look around the mountain to see what models and lengths of skis better skiers are using. Although there is invariably a good deal

The Ski Better Book

of fad and fashion involved—everybody likes to be on the current hot brand—the chances are that skis that do not measure up in quality and performance under the prevailing conditions at your area are not going to be seen in any quantity.

Length is a hard-to-make decision. All skiers, except racers, are using shorter, easier-to-turn skis than a few years ago. You seldom see anything much longer than 195 cm. But where skiers used to err on the side of too much length, they now err on the side of too little.

Longer skis are much more stable and ride the bumps more smoothly. At higher speeds, this is an important quality.

The table gives you an indication of proper length, based on your skill and weight, but pick the longer ski if the decision could go either way and if you are improving rapidly.

Between the test reports and your own random survey, you should be able to narrow down your choice to about two or three models. At this point, you can toss a coin and be reasonably certain of a good buy, but as much for your future needs as for immediate practical purposes, go one step further and conduct your own ski test by either renting or borrowing models you are considering buying. Many shops have demonstration skis of the most popular models they carry and most of the larger manufacturers have extensive on-the-hill demonstration programs that enable you to sample one or more of their skis for a couple of runs. You should take advantage of these opportunities whenever you can.

What should you be looking for on a demo ride? Basically, a ski is judged on its ability to track (maintain a given direction without shimmying from side to side), turn, and sideslip, and its behavior in the bumps at various speeds on soft snow, hard pack, and ice. A professional tester will wring the last ounce of performance out of the skis and will watch particularly their reaction to specific techniques and maneuvers. But at this stage these finer points need not be of particular concern to you. Aside from the obvious necessity that the ski track straight without shimmying from side to side, turn easily, hold on ice, and ride over the bumps without bucking at the highest speed you can muster, the characteristic you most need is the ability of the ski to forgive error and to accommodate a wide range of techniques. Some skis, particularly when combined with stiff boots, require extremely precise execution to function properly, and you should steer away from these models until you are really and truly an advanced to expert skier.

Simply because a ski does not quite measure up to your expectations on the first couple of runs, don't just dismiss it. Try to pinpoint the problem; sometimes the remedy is simpler than you think. If the ski seems to be all right except that it is hard to get into the turn, a somewhat shorter length may be the answer. If it consistently overturns or underturns, the source of the difficulty may be binding location—which is seldom calculated for your particular boots. Even if there is no cure, at the very least you know what you don't want and the ski salesman can steer you away from other models with similar characteristics and toward those more suitable.

After you've taken the plunge, don't expect instant magic. Although a pair of skis fresh from the factory should be ready for the slopes, the fact is that they seldom are. Like cars, they need to be tuned, which a conscientious ski shop will do but which you should really learn to do yourself. This comes under the heading of maintenance, treated in detail in Chapter 9. In the meantime, you should be aware that you didn't buy a bad pair simply because your skiing ability didn't immediately make a great leap forward. Usually, it takes a couple of days of hard skiing to adapt yourself to a new pair of skis and quite frequently it takes further fine tuning before you're able to get the most from them.

Bindings

Traditionally, bindings are something of an afterthought, probably because in skiing's Dark Ages they used to be simple bits of low-cost hardware—appropriately called bear traps—whose only function was to clamp the boots on the skis. In contrast, modern bindings can discriminate between a force that is about to break your leg and one that is supposed to turn your skis and can release, or not release, your leg as the situation requires. As usual with marvels of engineering, they cost a great deal more—about seventy-five dollars and up for the top models—but are still a lot cheaper than the medical repair bill for a fracture. Fortunately, the best is best for beginners and experts alike (with the possible exception of international-class racers). With reasonable maintenance they last almost forever. Barring a sensational breakthrough in the state of the art, you'll probably never need to change bindings again and can transfer them from ski to ski without trouble. It will probably pay you in the long run to buy the best you can afford right off the bat. Lower-cost models of the same brand will do about the same as the higher-cost version, but in addition to some high-end performance you may want a couple of years from now, you will also lose the high-quality finish that protects the binding from wear and tear and from the elements.

Buying bindings is becoming much simpler. Over the last few years, most foreign manufacturers have complied with European standards, which prescribe key parameters of binding performance. Even tougher and more far-reaching standards are being proposed by ASTM (American Society for Testing and Materials). The effect of all this activity is that virtually all poor bindings have been driven off the market and that you can be sure you'll be buying a binding that works, *providing you keep it properly maintained and adjusted.* Once the American standards are adopted, you'll be free to concentrate on the features you want without excessive concern about function.

There are now two basic types of bindings: plate and non-plate. The plate-type is a more recent development and appears to be gaining favor because binding function is independent of sole shape and condition—a vital factor in the older non-plate type—and because it allows ready exchange of boots, which makes it ideal for rental

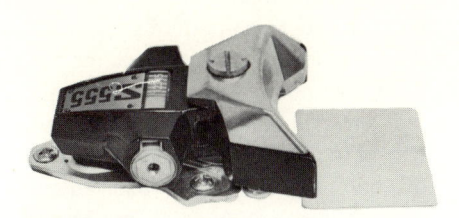

Until a few years ago bindings consisting of separate toe and heel units (a) were standard. They're still preferred by most performance-conscious skiers and provide a wide range of adjustment at both heel and toe. Plate-type bindings (b) are not as difficult to keep in adjustment since release function doesn't depend on the cleanliness of the boot. A new type of plate binding (c) is the ultimate in convenience. It retracts automatically after the need for release has passed.

purposes. However, the plates are not without drawbacks: they are invariably heavier, raise the boot fairly high off the ski, and since the plate is relatively rigid, they reduce the feel for the snow. As a general rule, most better skiers still prefer the non-plate binding; the plates are making their heaviest inroads among recreational skiers, particularly among those who became accustomed to them while they were still renting.

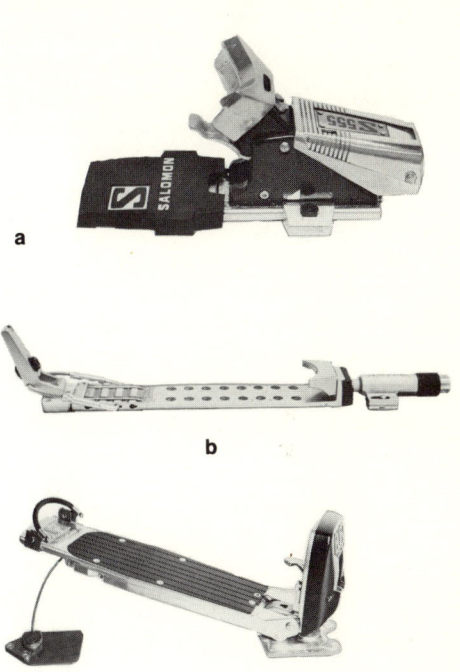

Most bindings currently on the market release in three directions: laterally to the sides at the toe and upward at the heel. There is probably a greater margin of safety with additional angles of release (see illustration), particularly upward at the toe under modern skiing conditions. But this has to be weighed against the risks of inadvertent release, which appear to increase slightly as the number of release angles increases, and the additional mechanical complications involved to make the binding function under high-performance conditions. For the moment at least, the battle is a standoff, but there is no doubt that bindings with more than three angles of release will gain as some of the mechanical problems are resolved and skiers become more safety-conscious.

Much more critical to the proper functioning of bindings is the need to minimize friction between boot and ski in non-plate bindings and between plate and ski in plate bindings. Friction between ski and boot or plate can reach tremendous levels in forward twisting falls and can make the binding almost useless unless some sort of anti-friction mechanism is present to allow the boot or plate to slide freely when the force against the leg approaches fracture levels. In plate bindings, this mechanism is usually built in, but in non-plate models —the type you are likely to inherit from a friend—a separate anti-friction pad is required. Most manufacturers now include a Teflon pad with their bindings, but practical and laboratory tests have now fairly well established that some of the more sophisticated mechanical devices, such as the Lipe Slider, perform better and more reliably, particularly under adverse conditions.

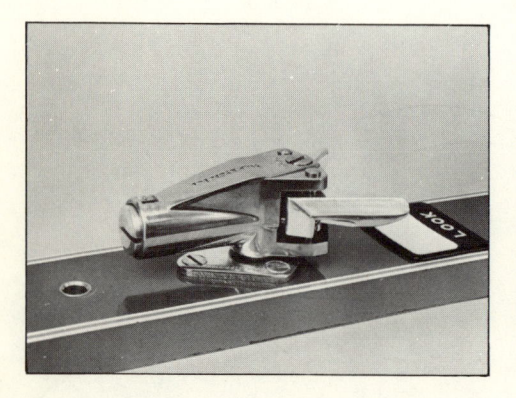

Bindings with separate heel and toe units need anti-friction pads under the ball of the foot to prevent friction between boot sole and ski from blocking the release mechanism. Most pads are of Teflon, as shown, but mechanical devices, which have two independent sliding surfaces, are more reliable and function even when there's dirt on the boot sole.

It is the ski shop's responsibility to make sure that the binding is properly mounted and functioning as designed. It is *your* responsibility to read the manufacturer's instructions and to make sure the bindings stay in adjustment and are carefully maintained. Admittedly, this is a somewhat tedious procedure, but it makes sense when you think of it in terms of mileage: you can't get much of it if you have a broken leg or a sprained ankle.

Poles

Pole lengths, like ski lengths, have shrunk slightly in the last few years. Inexperienced skiers should use poles about two or three inches longer than experienced skiers because they ski in a more upright stance and walk and climb more.

Buy quality poles using a high-grade aluminum alloy. The extra five to ten dollars between so-so and high-quality poles more than pays off in greater strength and resistance to bending, better rings and grips, and better finish.

Clothing

The way to keep warm on the slopes is not by piling on the heaviest sweaters, underwear, pants, and jacket you can find, but by dressing in several light layers that trap insulating dead air. If the weather warms up, you can remove one layer at a time until you feel comfortable.

Ski clothing is highly fashion-oriented these days, so unless you are into the fashion thing, buy good quality, timeless basics that will remain reasonably stylish for years to come.

If all ski slopes were smooth and gentle, balance and edge control would be sufficient to maneuver the skis—just like skating. However, ski terrain, with its convoluted bumps and hollows and its variations in pitch, is extremely complex and requires rapid turning. With the skis capable of accelerating swiftly to unmanageable speeds, waiting for nature to turn the skis is too slow a process to get you safely across the fall line. You have to take positive action to get the turn started.

This is called *turn initiation,* and you are already familiar with one element of it: the change of edges at the start of a turn. On well-groomed, easy trails, all you have to do is bank and change the edges, shift your weight to the outside ski as you do so, and then maintain sufficient edge angle and pressure so that nature can do its work.

On steeper, bumpier slopes this is no longer enough, and you actively have to twist the skis to initiate the turn. With shorter skis, this is no longer the chore it used to be. But when the skis are across the slope on edge, it is still difficult to twist because friction is too high. Furthermore, it is almost impossible to pivot the skis, as the back edges dig into the snow. Somehow you must momentarily reduce the grip of the edges so that you can twist the skis to get the turn started. Because your weight causes the edges to grip, you must unweight to release them.

Unweighting

There are several different ways of *unweighting,* depending on what you

Five
Turn
Initiation

mean by different. I mention this point because someone is forever inventing a new way to unweight. An instructor with aspirations to be a technique guru once spent an entire evening describing to me all the ways to unweight, about a dozen before I lost track. Actually they all boil down to *three* basic ideas. Since they all have their uses, you should be familiar with all of them.

(1) The bathroom-scale effect: When you stand on a bathroom scale and rise smartly from a knee-bent position, the scale will register a weight greater than your body weight until you stop rising; at that moment, the weight will drop almost to zero for a brief period before it again registers your normal body weight. You can achieve a similar effect by allowing your body to drop sharply, except in this situation, the weight will decrease during the downward motion and increase when you stop dropping.

You can achieve exactly the same effects on skis; they are called up-unweighting and down-unweighting. The hop that many ski schools use when teaching beginners and intermediates to ski parallel is a form of *up*-unweighting. However, in more advanced skiing, it is a much more subtle movement, a rhythmic down-*up*-down. In *down*-unweighting, the rhythm is up-***down***-up.

Up-unweighting is a bit simpler to do because it does not require such fine coordination of the other movements in turn initiation, as there is more time to get everything done than in down-unweighting. Down-unweighting is quicker because unweighting begins as soon as the motion starts and it has the additional advantage of lowering the skier's center of gravity at a moment when his balance is most precarious. All better skiers use both forms, depending on whether they are up or down at the moment they want to start their turn. An old instructor truism is that you have to be down to up-unweight and up to down-unweight.

(2) Use of terrain: Find a small bump and stand on it so that its top is directly under your feet. You can practically

For up-unweighting, approach the turn in a normal stance (a). As you get to the point of the turn, sink (b and c), then rise sharply (d). Note that the skis are almost completely off the ground in this sequence, although this isn't necessary to change edges and turn the skis.

Compared with up-unweighting, down-unweighting is usually much more subtle. You approach the turn in your normal stance (a), then execute a quick drop (b), during which you change edges and apply whatever turning force may be necessary. If you compare down-unweighting carefully with up-unweighting, you'll note that it's much quicker, and that there's no loss of snow contact.

spin the skis around since only the center of the ski is in contact with the snow.

Although there is no shortage of bumps and other breaks in the terrain where you can pivot the skis, do not go out of your way to unweight on them as many skiers, who suddenly discover this simplest way of unweighting, have a tendency to do. Let the situation as you find it in your normal descent be the guiding consideration in how you will unweight.

(3) One ski at a time: There is no law that says both skis have to be unweighted simultaneously. By putting most of your weight on one ski, you are free to move the other ski where you want it. You then put all the weight on the ski that has been moved and bring the now unweighted ski into position.

You can use a step straight to the side or slide the ski out tail first. The advantages of this method are twofold:

It is easy to coordinate with the other turn initiation movements, especially the change of edges.

It avoids that precarious moment in turn initiation when balance is marginal since one ski is always firmly planted.

Its disadvantage, when used too early in the learning process, is that it can lead to a stem habit which you will have trouble curing.

Pole Planting

The poles are skiing's jack of all trades. Aside from such uses as stabbing candy wrappers and warning that a skier is wounded when crossed and stuck in the snow, they are used as a balance aid, a timing device, and a turn coordinator. The pole—always the one on the *inside* of the turn—is brought into action by planting it in the snow.

49 Turn Initiation

a

b

Irregular terrain that frees the ends of the skis and leaves them suspended only in the middle makes it easy to pivot the skis into the new direction. Only the principle is illustrated here, but almost any kind of a break or bump in the terrain will serve.

Where in the snow is another one of those matters of feel and experimentation. It depends on speed, steepness of the slope, and radius of the intended turn.

Generally speaking, the pole should be planted **forward** of the boots and far enough to the side so the shock of impact, as you run up on the pole, can be absorbed by your elbow without your elbow being driven back into your ribs and knocking you off balance. The faster you are going, the farther forward you have to plant the pole. The tighter the turn, the more it has to be to the side. If you point the pole to the spot where you expect your skis to cross the fall line as you plant it, that will be about right for most of your turns.

Although the pole provides light support during turn initiation, its primary value is as a trigger to fire off the turn. You do not really lean on it or use it as though you were swinging around a fence post. The pole goes in and—zap—you unweight, change edges, twist your feet—and the turn is under way in a lot less time than it takes to read about it.

Turning Power

I have already mentioned that one of the ways to make skis turn is to twist the feet in the direction of the turn. This deserves some elaboration.

The Ski Better Book   50

One of the problems we encounter with twisting the feet with skis on edge and across the slope is that friction is too high. This is why we must unweight or at least flatten the skis against the snow. A second problem is that, when you are twisting just with your feet, there is only limited rotation.

You will get a much better appreciation of the latter difficulty, and of its solution, by standing flatfooted with knees straight on a smooth, hard floor. Just twisting with the feet does not get much action; it even feels weak. You can improve on that noticeably by standing slightly on the balls of your feet, even more by bending your knees slightly, and more yet by bending them a lot. Going through this demonstration in ski boots, which prevent the ankles from rolling, you will notice that by twisting with the knees, sometimes called **knee**

The stem christie is a form of unweighting one ski at a time. As you approach the turn (a), you shift weight to the downhill ski and set the now light uphill ski at an angle to the downhill ski by sliding its tail out to the side (b–c), a movement that is usually accompanied by downward motion. On the following up motion, the weight is shifted to the outside, angled ski (d), and the inside ski is slipped alongside and parallel to the outside ski. Stem turns can also be made by stemming with the downhill ski.

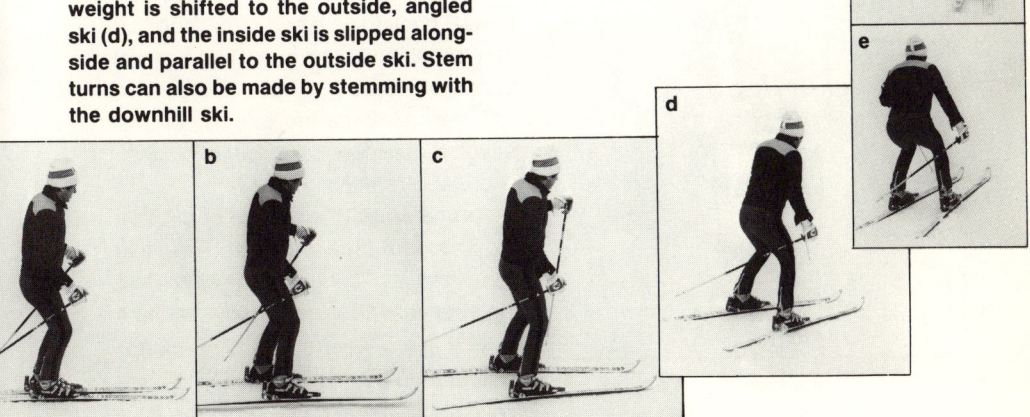

The radius of the turn you plan to make is the key to where to plant the pole. For a long-radius turn, the pole has to be planted fairly close to the front of the ski and only about a foot or so off to the side (a). For shorter radius turns, the pole has to be set closer to the boot and farther off to the side (b). The plant in (c) is either for an extremely tight turn or a stop turn.

Here are just about all the mistakes in pole planting in one picture (d). The elbow is too sharply angled and tucked in to the ribs, the pole is cocked inward, and these motions involve an awkward body position. If this were for real, the next photo would show the skier on his fanny.

crank, the boots roll from one edge of the sole to the other. If you were on skis you would get an edge change and a strong turning force simultaneously as is shown on page 51.

Twisting is a strong turning force, but in wet, heavy snow and in difficult terrain conditions, you need even more, particularly if you still use longer skis. You can reinforce the twist by one of several devices: anticipation, heel-push, and rotation.

Anticipation, the turning boost that most modern-style skiers use, has been described as "controlled downhill falling" because the upper body makes a tighter radius than the skis. It sounds scarier than it really is. Actually, it is exceptionally stable because all the turn-

The Ski Better Book 52

ing forces are generated **before** the skis begin to turn. Hence, **anticipation.**

Anticipation begins with a twisting of the upper body and the hips in the direction of the turn, the amount to be determined by the sharpness of the turn. When the body is sufficiently twisted, the pole is planted so it prevents the upper body from moving in the direction the skis are traveling. This causes the skis to shoot ahead in what is called **jetting** and reduces the pressure on the tips. At this moment the edges are changed by cranking the knees into the turn. Since the upper body is prevented from unwinding by the planted pole, the untwisting force is transferred to the legs and provides a powerful boost to turn the skis.

There are two critical aspects to anticipation:

> The skis must be kept on edge until they begin jetting to maintain the twist force.
>
> The pole plant must be made sufficiently downhill from the skis so that you will automatically bank (the downhill falling mentioned earlier).

Anticipation of a tough turn begins at the completion of the previous turn. With the skis still on their uphill edges (hidden in a, but still quite apparent in b), you twist your body in the direction of the turn coming up. The skis are prevented from turning because they're still on edge. As the skis run up on the bump, the pole is planted, preventing the upper body from untwisting. As the skis jet forward, the body being held back by the pole, they become light and the legs, assisted by knee crank, untwist in the direction of the turn. Turns can also be anticipated in less spectacular fashion.

53 Turn Initiation

Since present-day skis are designed to carve and minimize skidding, heel push is used only in the later phases of the turn by better skiers. To make the tails slide to the outside of the turn, release the edge and angulate more as shown. For an edge set, wait until you're well past the fall line before releasing the edge, then re-edge just before you plant the pole.

This twisting of the body and falling can be made even more emphatic with a sharp edge set, letting the tails of the skis slip a bit by releasing the edges and then re-edging sharply just as the pole is planted. The effect is something like hitting the brakes. The upper body twists more (see why below) and is almost literally bounced downhill and would be except for the planted pole.

The phenomenon of the upper body turning in a direction opposite to that of the turn *(counter-rotation)* is a natural consequence when you turn skis with your feet. The best explanation of it is the piano stool effect. If you sit in a swivel chair with your feet off the floor and swing your upper body in one direction, the lower body will swing in the opposite direction. The same thing would happen on skis if they were completely unweighted. However, except in a few unusual skiing situations, it is the turning of the legs and lower body that causes the shoulders to counter-rotate, not the other way around.

This was the source of considerable grief in the 1960s when the fashionable reverse-shoulder was prescribed. Skiers would practically twist themselves into pretzels to achieve the desired look, but nothing happened down at their feet.

The tendency of the upper body to

The Ski Better Book

counter-rotate is sharply increased by *heel-push.* You let the tails of the skis slide to the outside of the turn, or actively push them in that direction.

To compensate for the excessive bank angle, most experienced skiers use twisting angulation to keep their weight over the edges. This explains the illusion that they are turning their skis by turning their shoulder in the opposite direction.

Although most good skiers avoid heel pushing to minimize the possibility of skidding, it does have its uses in adjusting the radius of the turn once the edge change has taken place, providing it is not overdone. It is especially useful when you are turning into an area you can't see from where you start your turn, where you may have to make a sharp mid-turn correction, for a quick check if you have picked up too much speed as you are about to turn, and for making a tight uphill christie to come to a fast stop.

Technically, you now have all the elements needed in skiing—edge control, balance, the equipment, and the supplementary skills to make them effective in snow conditions and on any slopes you may encounter. Now, it is only a matter of *putting it all together.*

The heavy emphasis on basic skills and the disregard for maneuvers (snowplows, stem christies, parallel turns, etc.) shown in the previous chapters may seem strange. This is because many ski schools, having developed instruction methods in an era when slopes were ungroomed and beginners were on hard-to-turn long skis, continue to use the traditional progression, which starts with very slow braking maneuvers and only gradually works up to turns with free-sliding skis.

I don't mean to imply that instructors using traditional methods do not teach basic skills. They do, but only indirectly, their argument being that most maneuvers are now designed with the insinuation of basic skills in mind. The question is whether this indirect approach is desirable or even necessary.

Obviously, I don't think so. But since you are going to encounter this approach in many ski schools, you should understand the pros and cons.

The argument made for stemmed maneuvers—with skis in a V and on their inside edges—when you first learn to ski is that they are simple to learn and safe, enabling you to enjoy skiing even after a minimum of instruction. There is some truth to this, but it misses the point.

Habits Hard to Break

Stemmed turns are *too* simple. It is easy to fall into the stem habit, particularly if you aren't especially athletic. It's a defensive habit that's difficult to break once you have it and makes it almost impossible to turn fast enough to cope

Six
Getting the Turn and Yourself Together

with more difficult terrain involving higher speeds. Stems and snowplows are useful last resorts, when all else has failed, for getting around hard-to-grasp technical points, but not much else.

The safety argument is statistically highly suspect. It is true that inexperienced skiers get hurt more often than experienced skiers, but some of the evidence points to the highly dangerous tips-crossed fall as one of the major causes for this rate. Stemmed turns are safe, but only as long as their practice is carefully supervised. This shoots down the argument that they enable the novice skier to get around safely more quickly.

At one time there was sound reason for the various stemmed maneuvers to make novice skiers mobile. These reasons have evaporated with the development of flexible, strong, sophisticated skis in lengths as short as 150 cm for adults and low-cost, comfortable boots that can transmit your motions efficiently to the skis. If you have difficulty turning or can't get a grip on a problem, the answer is to go to shorter skis, not to stemming.

Become One with Nature

The argument between traditionalists and avant-garde is not only stem versus parallel, but also maneuver polishing for style's sake versus maneuvering to deal with whatever the mountain happens to throw at us.

Maneuvers for their own sake lead to pretty, intensely stylized skiing that is more ballet than outdoor recreation. That's fine—after a point. Most good skiers indulge in it. Freestyling or **hot-dogging** is a new phase of skiing that has in part developed around this idea. The problem for those just getting into skiing is that few have the time or money for the kind of polishing that makes stylish skiing truly satisfying. In any event, it puts the cart before the horse. No one is going to be impressed by a perfectly executed stem christie on easy terrain. Ski schools deprive us of one of the sport's greatest pleasures when they emphasize maneuvers of marginal or fleeting utility at the expense of basic skills which enable us to deal with terrain as we find it. Basic skills—not maneuvers—are the means of control and when you have them, they loosen up your skiing senses and become a part of nature. You feel the snow and the changes of pitch. You turn because your senses tell you it's time to turn. And the turn will be parallel or nearly so because your senses tell you it is the most efficient and sensuous way to turn.

Contrary to what you may fear, learning to ski by concentrating on basic skills instead of maneuvers does not involve long, dull practice sessions or keep you from having fun early in the going. Once you are aware of basic skills, you long to put them together into a strong, precise, positive turn.

Let's take a look now at how it's done —in outline form first:

Sequence of Events in a Turn

To make a turn, you prepare for it by:
 preparing to unweight,

preparing to plant the pole, and anticipating;

initiate it by:
　planting pole,
　unweighting,
　changing edges and
　applying turning power;

as snow contact is regained:
　shift weight to outside ski;

and adjust radius of turn by:
　changing edge angle
　and shifting and
　adjusting pressure.

Key Movement

It is worth noting, again, that the **edge change** is the key movement in the entire chain of events. All the unweighting, pole planting, and anticipating will not do any good unless it is accompanied by an edge change appropriate to the turn. In this context, it is obvious. Yet, in practice, the lack of a decisive edge change—timid execution of the change without re-edging enough once the change has taken place—is probably the major weakness in turns made by most novices and intermediates. An extreme manifestation of this problem is called "catching the outside edge," where the outside edge digs into the snow just as the turn starts and trips you sharply onto your ear. More likely, a weak edge change will result in a weak, imprecise, and slithery turn with only marginal control as the skis go through the fall line. In part, this may be caused by the lack of confidence in the ability to balance, particularly if you have just advanced to steeper or more difficult terrain. The lack of confidence is usually due to the higher speeds involved.

Exercises in Balance

Unless you do something about this key problem, you will have trouble making progress—wherever you happen to be at this particular moment. Some skiers get away with this weakness because they can guts out their lack of positive control over their skis on easier terrain. But it will catch up to them sooner or later—usually sooner.

Cure the problem at the outset with one or a combination of the following exercises:

(1) In making your turns, change edges consciously and actively by banking and rolling the knees in the direction of the turn in one continuous movement, making sure the skis are well on their edges (the edges on the inside of the turn) and are really biting into the snow at the completion of the turn and that your weight is on the inside edge of the outside ski at the completion of the motion, as in the three turns illustrated on pages 56, 57 and 58.

(2) If you have difficulty balancing during a strong edge change, try the above on a flatter slope where you can ski more in the fall line (where your traverses do not have to be so shallow, that is, so directly across the hill). This reduces the amount the skis have to be rotated to achieve edge change and makes balancing easier. Then build back up again using shallower tra-

59　Getting the Turn and Yourself Together

It's all together here: the basic parallel turn with pole plant (b), up-unweighting and edge change (c), transfer of weight to the outside ski and banking (d), and preparation for the next turn (h) as the skis begin to traverse. You can build on this turn, making it tighter, using it on steeper and more difficult slopes, and skiing faster as you gain proficiency. Using the alternate methods to unweight and adding turning power you'll soon arrive at . . .

The Ski Better Book

Quick fast turns down the fall line. What makes this possible is rapid knee crank from side to side and using the end of one turn to start the next. By skiing at speed and in the fall line, the skis turn easily and with minimal initiation effort. The ability to make quick turns at speed also gives you confidence for . . .

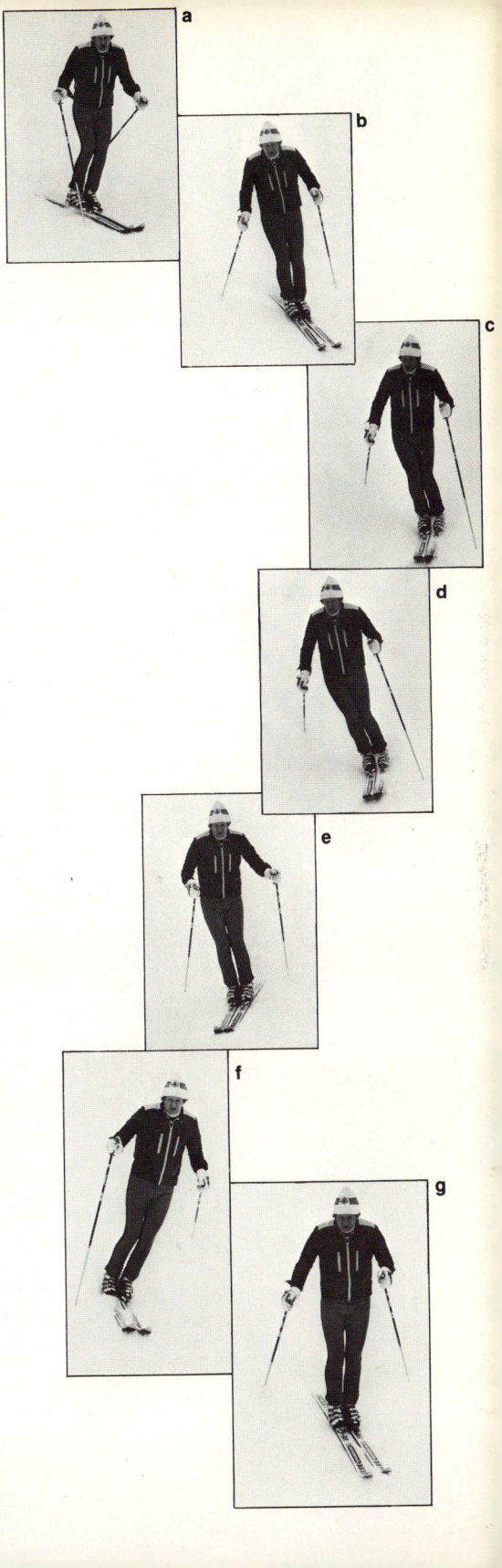

Romping in the big bumps. The trick among these maneaters is strong pole work, anticipation, and getting used to taking to the air. If you do become airborne, keep your knees loose and sink as you touch down to keep the shock from upsetting you. This little maneuver, incidentally, is currently the hottest thing in skiing and is called *avalement* (a French word meaning swallowing) for the way the shock bump is absorbed with the knees. Great skiing!

verses on somewhat steeper terrain. Use angulation (as shown on page 56) in slow, tight turns where centrifugal force is weak and where the angle of the edges is too great to bank the entire body into the turn, as on page 58.

(3) On steeper slopes, where the edge change requires a large rotation of the skis, use the pole as a balance aid by planting it just below the spot where you expect to change edges.

The Drawback

The drawback of turning with edge change only is that it confines you to the easiest slopes when you first start to ski. This is something of a problem in areas with restricted and narrow beginner slopes and easy intermediate trails. The solution is not to give up on the basic idea, but to supplement it with your sideslipping skills.

Instead of changing the edges quickly, as you would if you were in the fall line, release them as if you were going to sideslip and apply forward pressure. This slips the tips toward the fall line. If this slip is accompanied by a strong knee crank, there will be not only a sharp change of direction but an edge change as you keep the knee crank going.

Learning to turn this way is not quite as quick or as easy as the snowplow–stem-christie route, but edge change is such a vital element in all turns that it is absurd to worry about the extra time spent acquiring the skill. In any event, once you have achieved positive control over the edges, it is much easier to coordinate the other elements of the turn and you will be ahead in the long run.

As you get to steeper slopes, the need for pole planting, unweighting, and added turning power make themselves apparent. The effectiveness of these added elements in the initiation of the turn depends primarily on timing, which is a matter of practice, but also on a systematic approach. Add one element at a time, starting with pole planting, and integrate it into your bag of skills before going on to unweighting and anticipation. If you find that unweighting is not enough, for example, go back to an easier slope where you can turn with edge change and pole planting alone and work on unweighted turns there.

When adding a new element, always work on terrain you can handle to avoid resorting to defensive skiing just to complete the turn. To sharpen your skill in this new element, gradually increase the difficulty of the terrain, either by skiing more in the fall line or by going to steeper slopes.

Aim at Carved Turns

As your skiing improves, what you should aim for technically is a carved turn—a turn with no skidding of the skis.

There is some controversy among nitpickers whether this is technically feasible since there is a limit to the amount skis can bend into reverse camber, hence a limit on how tight an arc they can make without at least some skidding. But there is no debate about the desirability of reducing skid to a minimum. Carved turns are faster and

63 Getting the Turn and Yourself Together

more stable. Although speed may be of only marginal interest to you, stability is ever more critical as you get into steeper and more difficult terrain where skis accelerate rapidly and a skid can quickly degenerate into a spin.

If you have gotten into the habit of making a positive edge change to start a turn, there is no difficulty in starting a carved turn. The difficulty is in maintaining the carve, since the pitch of the slope and the forces acting on the skis are constantly changing.

As the skis accelerate toward the fall line, centrifugal force increases and will break the grip of the edges on the snow if the skis are not sufficiently edged or, because of unequal pressure distribution, either the tip or tail is too lightly weighted.

As the turn progresses, it usually requires a simultaneous increase in the edge angle. Because most turns are started with forward pressure, it also requires a shift of pressure from the front to the center and sometimes to the back of the ski. This is easier said than done since every model of ski reacts slightly differently and because of the many variations in slope, acceleration, and speed that may occur.

It takes a fine feel for the edges to maintain a carve. You can usually feel whether you are carving or skidding, but the ultimate test is a look at the track. If it looks as though it had been made by a windshield wiper, you are not carving. A carved turn leaves tracks that seem almost scribed into the snow.

Error Detection and Correction

So far, we have assumed all is going well. Unfortunately, this is rarely the case, especially in the very early stages. You will fall, probably often at first. More insidious, the turn you had planned does not come off as you intended. It is important for you to know what went wrong so you can correct the cause of the error.

It is not always so easy. If your turn begins to degenerate as you approach the fall line and the skis want to go straight downhill instead of curving across the fall line, it may seem that you did not make a complete edge change. But when you edge the skis more, they are still slow in coming around. Could it be that you are leaning so far back that there is not sufficient pressure on the skis to keep them bent into reverse camber? Maybe, but you felt your shins pressing against the front of your boots before you started the turn! Then it could be that the way you planted your pole shoved you backward, which, in turn, might have been caused by a pole too long (most beginners and intermediates are supplied with poles about two inches longer than advanced skiers because they usually ski in a higher stance).

You see why novices and low intermediates are discouraged from trying to teach themselves. They are not experienced enough to trace back to the real source of their problem. Frequently, they are not even aware that something that is not supposed to happen has happened. They learn that they have erred only when the maneuver ends in a fall. Symptom analysis, such as: "Damn! I lost my balance" or "I caught an edge" does not solve the problem. You may have to back up several stages to find the real cause.

Trace the Problem to Its Source

Error analysis, though not easy, becomes less difficult if you are basic-skill conscious because you are more apt to be aware of the proper attitude of the skis and body in relation to one another and the slope. This enables you to trace the problem to its source as we did above. Or by reversing the process by which you learned, you can determine the general area of your difficulty. For instance, suppose you've arrived at the unweighting stage, but as you attempt to turn with unweighting on more demanding slopes, your balance becomes precarious and the turn no longer comes off smoothly. Is the problem the way you unweight and the way you time the movement with pole plant and edge change? You can experiment with that possibility and find the solution right there. But you may not, in which case you should go back to a slope where you can turn with pole plant and edge change only and check yourself out. Critically, because the demands on your edge and balance skills are much greater at higher speeds. Is the combination of edge change and pole plant really as sharply and smoothly executed as it should be? Do you have to fudge in little ways, like lifting a shoulder to get past the pole, or has your arm a tendency to drag behind you as you withdraw the pole? If so, this may be your real problem in unweighting. Work on the planting of the pole, but don't overlook the possibility that there may be something wrong with the way you change edges and bank that causes you to rely on your pole for more than just momentary support.

An error as such, even if it results in a fall, is nothing to worry about; it happens all the time, even to the best of skiers. However, if an error keeps recurring, it's time for a lesson. An instructor can watch you ski and is specifically trained in error detection and correction; he can help you regardless of the teaching method he happens to use. Don't be too proud and waste too much time before you seek his help.

Some Common-Sense Ideas

Up to now, I've discussed skiing in almost purely technical terms. This is essential if you are learning. However, don't lose your perspective. Skiing is an outdoor activity and it should be fun and should stimulate the instincts we have no opportunity to use in our sheltered nine-to-five existence. Before I continue along technical lines, let's look at skiing from a wider horizon.

Stay in Shape. Of course you have to be in shape! Sliding down a hill doesn't seem very demanding physically, but it is, and if you're not in condition, it will slow your progress to a snail's pace. Personally, I dislike exercise regimes intensely, but if you've allowed yourself to slip, a tough, daily regime is the only solution. Once you're back in shape, make sure you stay that way by playing tennis, soccer, or other physically demanding games. As former U.S. Ski Team Coach Willy Schaeffler once told me, "Don't get in shape to ski, get in shape to live."

Be Adaptable. It cannot be stressed enough—and perhaps it should be called the First Fundamental—that skiing is a sport of an infinite number of variables. Sun, snow, temperature, and wind can substantially change a slope from one day to the next and, more subtly, from hour to hour. Move your starting point over a foot, and the difference can be as day is to night. Even if it were technically feasible to retrace a given track exactly, it would not be the same; simply by skiing on a patch of snow you change its character.

Because of the many variables in skiing, avant-gardists have maintained there is no such thing as *a* parallel turn, but only an infinite number of turns made with the skis parallel. Conceded, that's a bit fussy, but there's no argument about their basic point: You have to adapt to the specific requirements of the terrain since it obviously can't be vice versa.

Look Ahead. One of the ways of adapting to the terrain is to know what you are getting into. "Look ahead" is one of the more ancient bits of advice—skiing's equivalent to "keep your eyes on the ball"—and is a habit essential for survival. For the inexperienced skier it is important because neither reflexes nor technical skills are sharp enough yet to enable him to ski out of trouble. For the experienced skier, who has these capabilities, it remains important because of the speeds at which he skis. At about 30 mph, not an unusually high speed during acceleration on steep slopes, there is less than a second to react to an obstacle 40 feet away. Why court disaster when it isn't necessary? Save those sharp reflexes for genuine emergencies.

Ski Relaxed. This always gets a good chuckle, but being tense to the point where your muscles grow rigid can cross up your nervous system. If the bumps and ruts start catching you by surprise or if you cannot feel the skis react, you are too tense. Fear is the greatest source of tension; prolonged extreme effort is the other. To relax, stay off slopes that scare the hell out of you, slow down, or rest.

Don't Be Over-Technical. This could also be stated *don't take it too seriously*. After you've been concentrating on improving for a while, change the routine and pace by skiing purely for the fun of it. Too large a dose of exercising can get to be a bore, which actually slows down learning. Give your senses a chance to absorb the new knowledge.

Keep Working on Improvement. This may seem to contradict the above, but there usually comes a point—invariably when you've learned to make reasonably proficient turns on the more interesting intermediate terrain—when skiing becomes so much fun that it is hard to get serious about learning more. Resist this urge, not only because it circumscribes your skiing possibilities—particularly on larger mountains, where trails may not always be purely intermediate—but also because the vagaries of the weather can turn that fun trail into an expert skating rink. This may ground you after you've paid for the trip to the area; it could also result in injury. Both for fun and safety's sake become the best possible skier you can.

Ski Dynamically. One of the problems with instruction is that it breaks down what is really one continuous motion into separate parts. This makes you self-conscious, constantly thinking where your poles, skis, and your body are, and breaks up the rhythm of the turn itself and the rhythm as you swing from one turn to the next. You have to cultivate spontaneity by relaxed skiing.

To use the tennis analogy: a good player does not say to himself, as the ball comes over the net, I will use a backhand; he uses it because, through experience, he has learned to recognize the situation without thinking about it. Spontaneously, he reacts accordingly. Since he does not worry about the kind of stroke he is about to make, he is free to concentrate on the ball and where he wants to place it. Similarly, if you ski spontaneously, you are free to concentrate on the terrain and react accordingly.

That's It!

With the basic skills mastered you can refine your turns. But skiing has an element of mystery, that uncertainty of what the terrain has in store for you. Refinement of a turn depends on the terrain and how you can cope with it and your ability to analyze your errors in dealing with it.

I have made passing references to bumps, sudden sharp changes in pitch, trees, and various types of snow conditions. How do you go about handling the problems they create?

Because terrain is so variable, there is little that can be said about it in the abstract. It does not help to tell you to make sharper turns and more of them on steeper terrain or to turn around bumps. Exactly what you do depends on your capabilities at any given time. What you might carefully ski around at the beginning, you might take straight later on. You must use judgment, which you can, in part, acquire by watching other skiers of your skill level trying the same thing, but mostly by doing it yourself.

Before tackling a slope with which you are not familiar, study it (see illustrations of various types of slopes) and map out an approximate route down. Even the most difficult slopes always have some places where they are easy, smooth, or flat enough for less than super skiers to manage a turn. Pick these out and traverse between them. After you have skied this man-eater a couple of times, you will find other places which, at first, seem impossible for turning but are really quite easy. For instance, huge bumps are awesome at first, but in some cases you can ski around their perimeter and completely change direction without an edge change.

You'll ultimately be more successful in dealing with difficult terrain if you stay as close as possible to the fall line and ski it as you find it. Turning down the hill from a traverse almost straight across a very steep slope requires a hair-raising

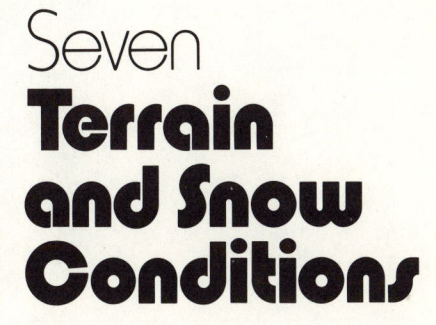

Seven
Terrain and Snow Conditions

a

b

(a) Although steep in spots, this slope is so wide that even inexperienced skiers can handle it by weaving back and forth in speed-killing traverses.

(b) Curvaceous, loaf-shaped, and friendly bumps. There is room to ski between them, and even if you ride across one, you can pivot your skis at its crest and slide down the other side.

(c) Another steep slope with a saving grace. By sliding down one side of the gully and riding up the other, you can slow down enough to turn with fairly nominal skills. But don't get as high up on the wall as the fellow on the upper left did. He's going to have quite a time getting down unless he skis against the general flow of the traffic.

initiation, and it's much easier to make quick, successive linked turns to control speed than to turn the skis too much across the fall line. As you pick up turning proficiency, cultivate the habit of staying in the fall line and only move up to steeper slopes as you master fall-line descent. This doesn't mean you have to make short turns down the hill in all situations, but the opportunity for making long, swinging turns on more difficult slopes is rare these days. Heavy skier traffic creates moguls (the bumps skiers make by turning on the same spot) faster than grooming machinery can knock them down.

The problems of different snow conditions can be dealt with more specifically.

Ice and Deep Snow

The problem with *ice* is that the skis turn too readily and the grip of the edges is easily shaken loose if maximum pressure isn't maintained on the edges at all times. To ski ice, sharpen your edges, make the initiation of the turn as smooth and gentle as you can, and maintain maximum edge pressure at all times to prevent skidding.

If you've cultivated your carving skills, a big portion of your battle against ice is already won since the secret of skiing ice is to avoid skidding and loss of edge contact. If ice conditions are extreme—blue and boilerplate in skiing vernacular—the use of lateral projection will help to maintain edge contact during edge change. In lateral projection—which is one-leg-at-a-time unweighting—all the weight is first shifted to the downhill ski so that the uphill ski can be moved slightly to the side and onto its inside (of the turn-to-be) edge. Then the weight is shifted laterally (not with an up-motion) to the uphill ski. This eliminates the mo-

Mean wicked bumps with seemingly no easy route through. Great only for those who've mastered *avalement* . . .

. . . And those who haven't wait for the snow-grooming machine.

mentary loss of firm edge contact during initiation and minimizes the period when there is no significant pressure on at least one of the edges. An incidental benefit is that lateral projection widens the stance during the most unstable point of the turn. Lateral projection need not be confined to ice, but it does require an athletic approach to skiing.

In very soft, soggy snow and deep powder, the problem is just the reverse. There's no lack of edge contact, but with the snow yielding readily, pressure on the skis is not high enough to bend them into reverse camber. However, by going fast enough so that the pressure of the snow against the tip forces the ski to plane (float) in the snow—the tips don't have to ride above the snow for that purpose—we can make the skis turn by banking. In this situation, the tip compresses the snow ahead of the ski and creates a banked track that is, momentarily, just strong enough to make the skis curve into a turn. With stiff skis it takes a great deal of speed to make the tips plane, but skiers who have lots of opportunities to ski deep powder usually have a specially soft-flexed model that emphasizes the ability to plane.

Skiing deep, trackless snow is an absolutely euphoric but touchy exercise. Speed must be maintained and the

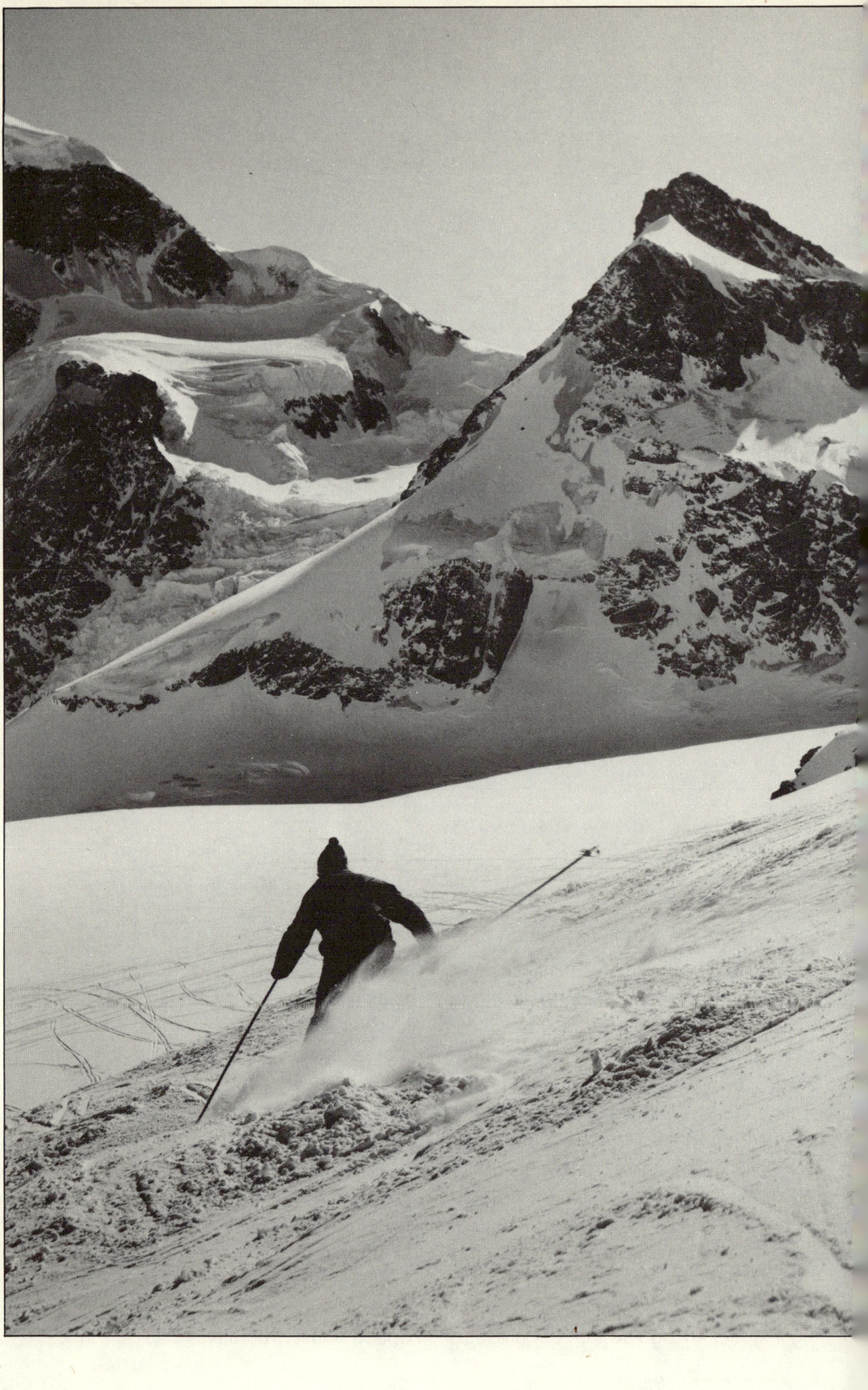

From a distance, the virtually unskied snow below the skier at left looks good, but it could be deceiving. If the snow were good, the tracks wouldn't be quite so sharply etched. It's probably breakable crust, which is a very hairy snow condition for experts. Better follow the packed trail if you're not one.

The ultimate nightmare. Old frozen tracks below, breakable crust on the other side of the ridge, and a staircase for a trail. The only answer is to catwalk back and forth down the stairs and make sure you don't take the same trail again.

turns have to be made in the fall line to prevent the speed from dropping to the point where the skis fall off the plane. Weight must also be carefully distributed equally between both skis so they maintain the same level of plane. If one planes more than the other, the skis take different tracks or the more heavily weighted ski dives. Once the skis take divergent paths, it's difficult to correct the situation; since the problem is cumulative, you'll end up with snow in your ear.

It's hairy, but, oh, what fun!

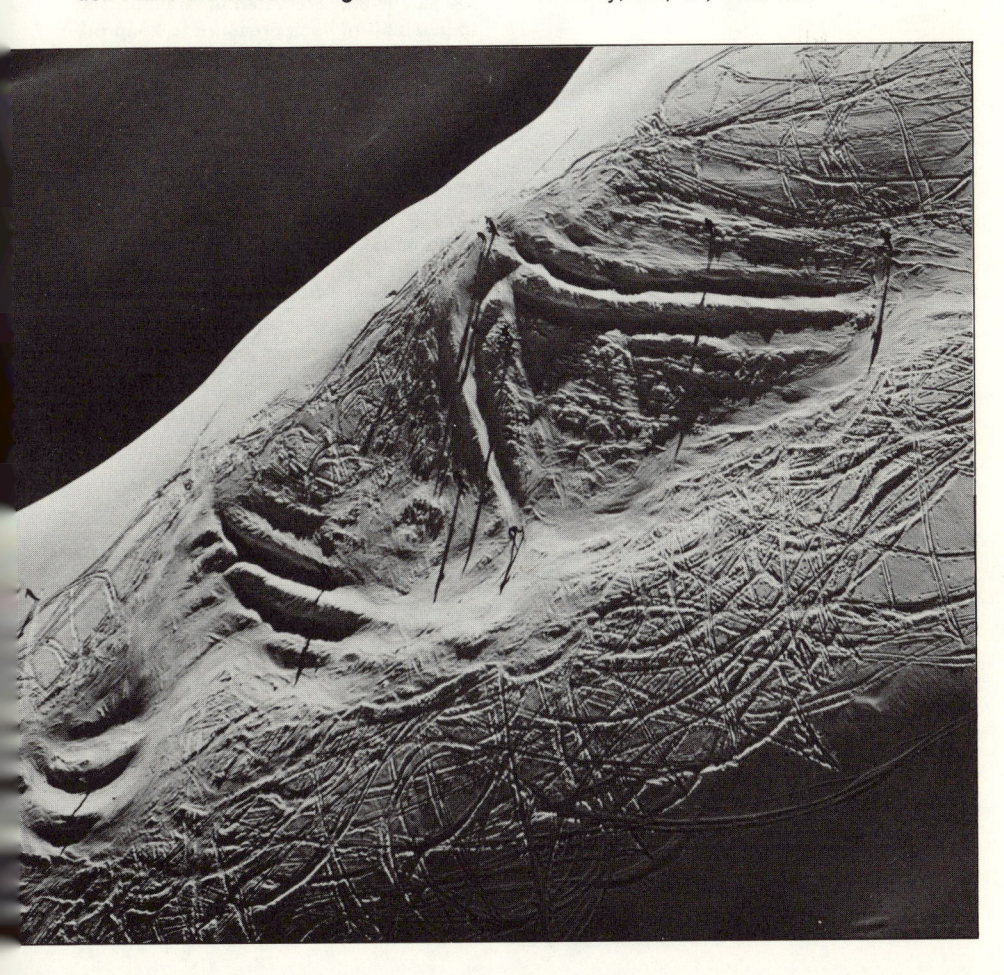

Look carefully at this deep powder sequence and compare it with the jet turn with *avalement* on page 62. If you can visualize the skis in the snow, you'll find remarkable similarities in the sequences. Pick up speed first by skiing straight down the hill so the tips plane out of the snow (a), then plant the pole (b)—sort of a light jab—to trigger a bank and a slight turn out of the fall line. As soon as the skis begin turning, prepare to come back to the fall line (c) with a bit of anticipation and another pole plant. This allows the skis to jet to the surface (d), and you immediately bank into the next turn. The secret to skiing deep powder is to keep the skis evenly weighted at all times and to use a bit of back pressure to keep the tips on or near the surface. Soft, flexible skis also help, although powder skiing with short skis is becoming immensely popular.

If you're a powder skier, you know exactly what's going on. If you're not and try to muddle through by skiing where it has been skied out, don't. Cut powder is more difficult to ski than uncut, particularly if it has set up a bit. Furthermore, powder skiers seek out the steepest pitches. You follow their tracks at your own peril.

The Ski Better Book 76

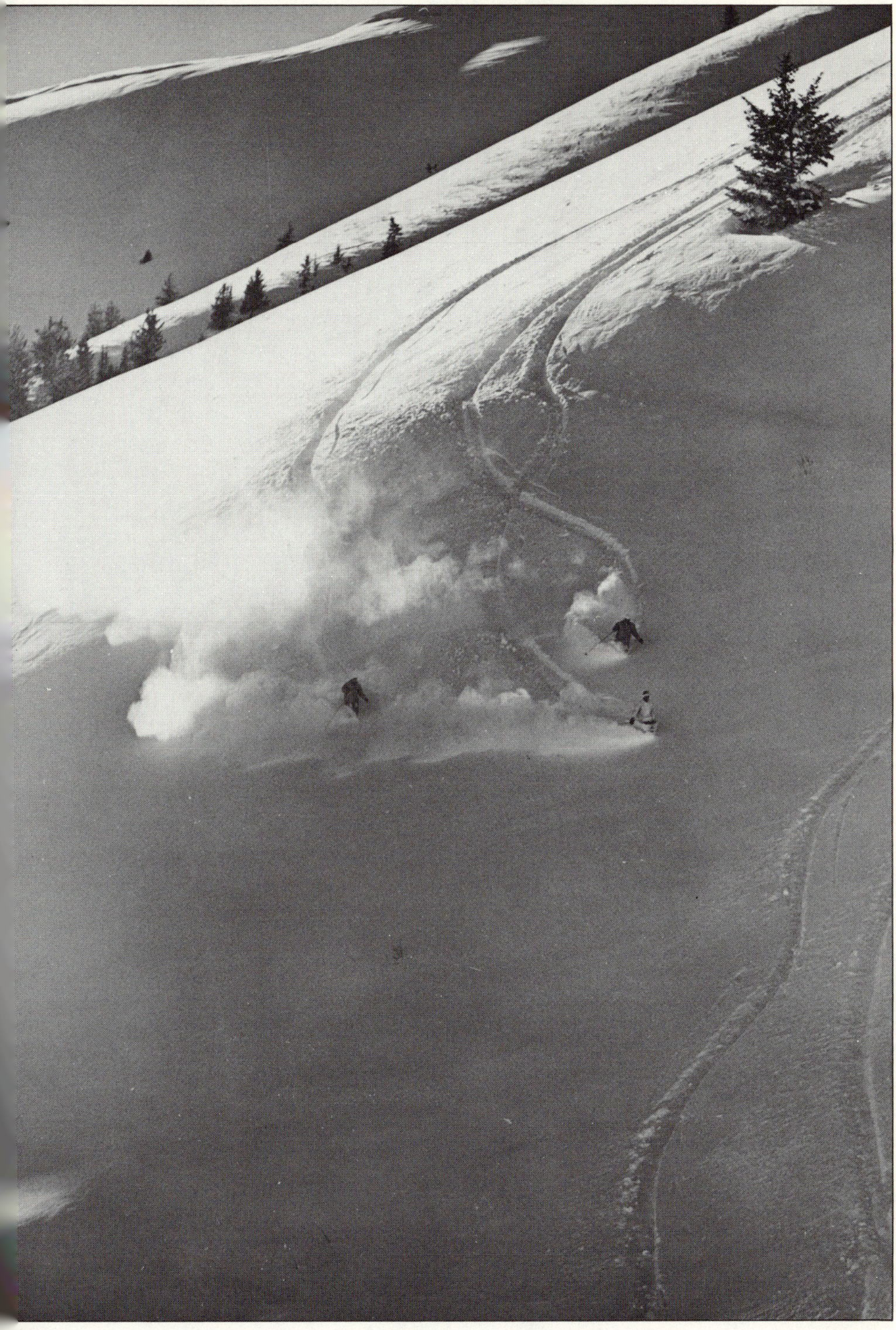

Skiing can be a scary sport. You probably do not have to be reminded of this, but with the advent of reliable release bindings, there has been an increasing tendency to overstate skiing's safety and a corresponding temptation to put you down for your fears. You are not alone in your fears. Remember, always, that your instincts are a better guide to the situation than the hustle of skiing entrepreneurs or the more insidious assurances of your well-meaning skiing friends that your fears are groundless.

Although it is true that improvements in equipment, instruction, and slope grooming have greatly reduced the chances of a broken leg, the danger of trees, rocks, and avalanches is still with us. With the number of skiers growing every year, some new hazards have cropped up: skiing speeds are increasing, the collision potential is greater, and moguls are more difficult to handle.

Skiing is risky but not unsafe. Researchers in preventive medicine are finding that calculated risk-taking is part of human nature and a healthy exercise both mentally and physically. Taking a calculated risk and succeeding is a stimulating and occasionally euphoric experience. That is why skiing, with its risks, is such a satisfying sport.

Eight
Psyching Up for Skiing

Some Snags

Calculated risk-taking, it must be stressed, is not reckless. By combining technical skill, good equipment, and experience, you can overcome the risks. Working up to more difficult trails gradually, within your capabilities, you can increase the risks you take, but safely.

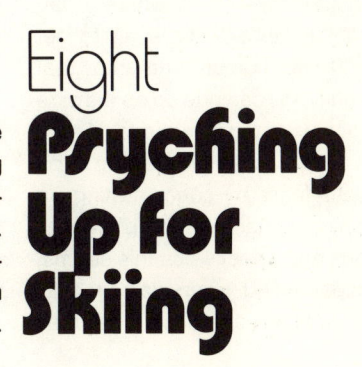

This sounds reasonable, but there are some snags. Nature did not endow every ski area with trails and slopes perfectly graded for every increment of skill. Periodically, it throws curve balls, such as blue ice, hip-deep powder, and breakable crust, which can scare even expert skiers. You might as well face it, at various points along the line you will be confronted with situations that call for going beyond what prudence dictates.

And you are afraid.

No one has made a catalogue of all the things that skiers fear, but most of them are obvious: falling, excessive speed, loss of control, being hurt, and being humiliated. These have been with us since childhood and no amount of reassurance from others will make them go away. You have to convince yourself that you can make it. You have to **psych yourself up**.

Positive Alternatives

Although every person has his own way of psyching himself up, the process basically involves overriding your fears with positive alternatives. "Yes, this section is steep, narrow, and bumpy," you tell yourself, "but I can traverse to that flat spot over there where I can turn. Then I can sideslip a bit to get through those bumps and into that smooth gully so I can ride up on the side to slow down or stop if I need to." Many times it is just as simple as that. You forget your fears by concentrating on the technical aspects of the problem.

Obvious and effective as this seems, many experienced skiers fail to avail themselves of this approach. They may be rattled and are not thinking clearly, but more than likely, they have some preconceived notion of how a difficult trail should be skied and how they should look skiing it. This is an affliction that seems to strike skiers who have just graduated into parallel with special ferocity. They get it into their heads that wide traverses, sideslipping, and using easy outs is bunny stuff and that they will lose status by resorting to them.

The Worst Fear

In other words, they are afraid of being humiliated. Too frequently this is a more powerful fear than all the others combined, particularly when one is skiing with a group. This feeling may be natural, but if you succumb to it, there is a triple-barreled penalty:

You will probably fall, so severely, perhaps, that all your fears will be aroused to fever pitch.

The value of the experience of skiing a more difficult slope will be wiped out.

Psychologically, you will be back at point zero and will have to go through the process of building your confidence all over again.

Facing Skibender

You can substantially set your fears to rest by taking a lesson or two whenever you are about to take another step forward or when you are at a strange ski area. But even more satisfying is to

The Ski Better Book 80

carefully set the stage for your next act of courage. Though you cannot be sure you are up to it, you feel the time has come to run Skibender, the trail for advanced skiers at your favorite area, which you have never skied.

First of all, do not act on your feelings immediately. Let the thought slosh around in your head for the rest of the day while you ski your usual runs. Try to ski faster than normal, attack bumps and other obstacles more aggressively, and reduce your number of stops. This will help to get you in the mood for what is to come.

That evening, prepare your skis carefully. Check the bindings, fill the gouges in the bottoms, sharpen the edges, and wax the skis (Chapter 9, "Ski Maintenance"). Get a good night's sleep.

In the morning, try to be among the first on the hill so you will have lots of room for your warm-up runs. Pick an easy slope for you, preferably one with a long, flat outrun so you can schuss it fast to get the feeling of speed. Then try something more difficult, but still well within your capabilities. This warm-up should tell you whether you are on the up-beat or not. If you feel you are not skiing well, there is no point in tempting fate.

If all is going well, you are now ready for Skibender. As you ride up on the lift, study the trail carefully wherever it is in view. Note how others ski it, but without making too much of the particulars. Watch the general flow of traffic and try to pinpoint the hairiest places and possible ways around them. When you get to the top, do not be in a rush to shove off. Look at the scenery; that is an important part of skiing, too. Wait until the trail is reasonably clear before starting down.

Ski well below your normal speed. This is going to be an exploratory trip and the idea is to learn something about the trail, not to see how far you can get before you reach your technical limits. Stop whenever you feel yourself speeding up or when you get to a blind spot. Do not hesitate to sideslip to get over a difficult section. Look back periodically to see how other skiers are handling particular situations, compare their way with yours, and try to imagine what you would do the next time. In this fashion, gradually work your way to the bottom of the trail.

If you were able to manage, however crudely, you should go up for a second try even if the first trip was not particularly enjoyable. Hacking your way down is not much fun, but now that you have experienced Skibender, you know roughly what you are up against. Still at minimum throttle, but hopefully with more continuity, you will have ascertained whether your problems, if any, are a matter of getting used to Skibender's difficulties or whether you need more work on fundamentals.

Careful programming is especially useful when you are still in the process of nailing down the basics. Essentially, that is what ski schools do, but you can tailor the program to your own specific needs and pace. Your first attempt to ski something more difficult may be inconclusive. You may actually have to cut over to an easier trail. But if you programmed your attempt carefully, the experience should not be so traumatic as to discourage you. At the very least, you will have a realistic evaluation of your skiing skill and what you need before making the next attempt. Make careful note of what you are lacking and try to find situations on easier slopes where you can work on your weaknesses with a greater margin for error.

The Hazards of Slope Doping

The psychological hazards of more difficult trails are obvious. Except for a few brainless among us, most of us do not need much persuading to do the sensible thing when faced with such a situation. However, we would be less than human if we did not succumb to what I call **slope doping,** the tendency to simply slide up and down easier trails without making a conscious effort to improve. In some respects, this is a much more serious psychological hazard than the others mentioned previously because it is so subtle and seems such a lot of fun at the time.

There are far more temptations to slope dope than to scare the wits out of yourself on tough trails. Ski area managers are not fools and they know that a good set of intermediate trails is like money in the bank. They try to offer so much of this type terrain to assure you a good time. They may groom it to a fare-thee-well.

I am not against well-groomed intermediate slopes or skiing just for the fun of it, but the risk is that you will forget you want to become a good skier. Skiing under ideal conditions can be so comfortable at this stage of the game that you will simply stop progressing.

This may not seem much of a problem if most of your skiing is done at an easy area and there is nothing with more challenge nearby. But presumably, one day you will want to ski some of the great mountains in the Rockies or in Europe. You will only get the most out of such an adventure if you are a good skier. On a more mundane level, a sudden change in the weather right at home can turn those comfortable intermediate slopes into expert ice rinks. At the very least, you will be out a day of skiing. At worst you may suffer a painful fall.

If you have trouble pushing yourself to improve, the best way to solve the problem is to take a lesson in a fast class or ski with one of your more expert friends and try to keep up with him. Another way is to run slalom gates or to sign up for one of the fun races that most ski areas stage. This approach has many advantages discussed in Chapter 10: "The Uses of Racing and Cross-Country Skiing."

Nine
Ski Maintenance

I have stressed the need for good equipment, but much of what I hear blamed on poor skis is actually caused by a lack of maintenance. If you own a pair of skis, I am willing to wager that I can improve their performance by at least 50 percent in less than ten minutes.

Don't Let It Throw You!

Most skiers neglect to maintain their skis because they are afraid it is too complicated. Actually, it is nothing of the sort, even in extreme cases of neglect. In fact, you can partially and temporarily restore badly abused skis simply by coating the bottoms with hot wax and flattening them out with a ski scraper. If you prefer, you can have a ski shop do it for you. However, if you hot-wax your skis regularly from the time they are new or freshly reconditioned, you will need little maintenance other than occasional sharpening of the edges and filling in the gouges after you have run over a rock.

Another reason skiers neglect their skis is that they are under the false impression that polyethylene bottoms do not need wax because they already slide so well. The fact is, snow is surprisingly abrasive and, if left untreated, even the toughest bottoms will wear and stop sliding and turning smoothly.

Wax should be applied to skis that are dry and at room temperature. This permits a better bond between the wax and the polyethylene and prevents the wax from wearing off too quickly. The wax should also be appropriate for the anticipated snow conditions (instruc-

Hot-Waxing Skis

Melt the wax on an old iron and dribble it down the length of the ski.

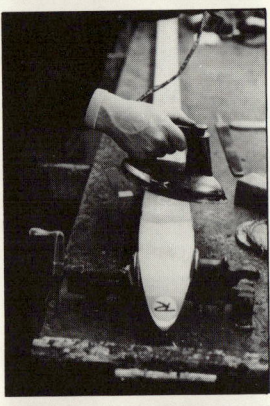

Smooth it out so that the bottom is completely coated.

Scrape excess wax out of groove with a scraper the shape of the groove.

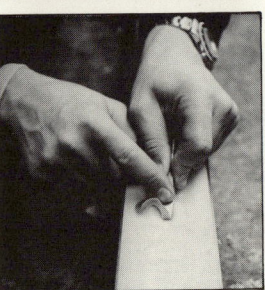

Scrape excess wax off bottoms with a cabinet scraper, leaving only a thin coat.

tions are on the package) to improve gliding and turning qualities. This is particularly important in spring when wet, granular snow will slow unwaxed skis.

Do It Yourself

Despite the best of care, edges will eventually become dull and ski bottoms will gouge and wear. You can leave that kind of heavier maintenance to your ski shop. But if you are at all particular, you will find that *you* can do a better job at lower cost. Ski shops will do a workmanlike job, but at five dollars and more an hour for a good shopman, they will try to keep hand labor to a minimum. Since it takes handwork to tune skis finely, either be prepared to pay at least ten to fifteen dollars to get the job done, or learn to do the job yourself.

There are a number of devices on the market to simplify filing the bottoms and sharpening the edges. Unless you are a skilled hand with a file, you are better off with one of these devices, as a perfectly square edge is absolutely essential for good performance. The best of these devices is Ski Tül, which is actually a special file holder that makes it possible to file both sides and bottoms even without a vise. A few strokes with the Ski Tül every two or three outings is usually enough to keep the skis in prime condition at all times.

For recreational skiers, the Ski Tül is by far the most convenient tool to file both the bottoms (a) and sides of the edges (b) without getting them out of square. Finish edges with emery paper to remove burrs.

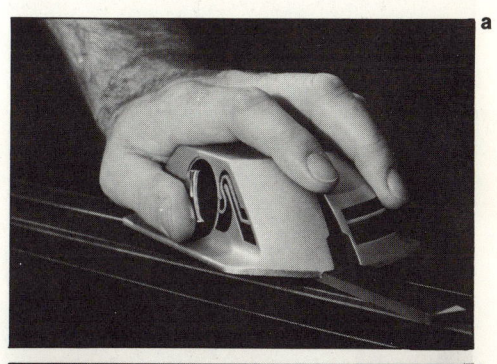

85   Ski Maintenance

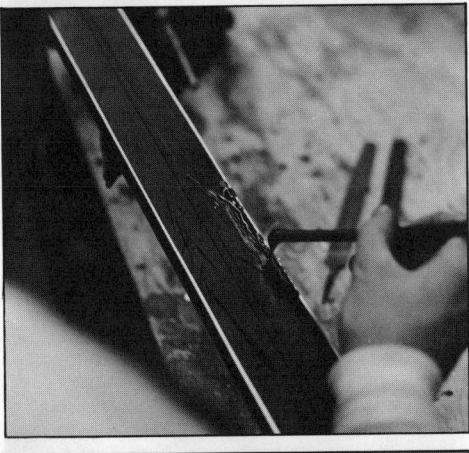

After cleaning skis, light candle and allow it to burn until it drips freely.

Keep candle close to the gouge to be filled to prevent new base material from oxidizing and forming a poor bond with the damaged area. Overfill the hole so there's something extra to smooth off.

Rasp off excess carefully and finish the bottom perfectly flat and smooth with emery paper.

The only real problem remaining is filling in gouges. This is done by means of a candle of the same color and material as the bottoms of your skis. Before you get started, make sure the skis are dry and at room temperature and clean the area to be repaired with wax remover.

REMEMBER: acetone, thinner, and gasoline are dangerous since you will be working with an open flame.

Light the candle and fill the gouge with the drippings. Keep the candle close to the work and move it along with each drop. Allow the material to cool and shrink. If it does not completely fill the hole, go over the area again. When the damaged area is large and so deep that the body of the ski is exposed, *first* seal the ski body with epoxy. After the epoxy has set, fill the area as described.

After this stage, the job looks like a mess, but don't let that worry you. Level off the repaired area with a rasp or a Stanley Surform (a rasp-like device available in every hardware store), then apply the finishing touch: first, with medium-to-coarse emery paper, then with fine. Use a sanding block or a flat piece of metal to keep the bottom flush and level. Rewax before using the skis again.

When you get out on the hill, it is entirely possible that the edges will be too sharp, which makes the skis squirrely and hooky. It is a good idea to carry a small stone or some emery paper to take off the microscopic burrs that are characteristic of an edge too finely drawn. You can use it also to knock off edge burrs which come from running over rocks.

Immeasurable Savings

You can save yourself endless problems, time, money, and unwanted ski-season time-outs by doing the following after every day of skiing:

(1) Clean up and dry off skis.

(2) Test the bindings for proper function and adjustment. Use a test device, if one is available. If you suspect something is wrong, have the bindings tested. Make sure the binding screws are tight.

(3) Inspect for delaminations and other possible damage to the body of the skis.

(4) Check the bottoms for gouges, scratches, and wear, particularly where the edges and the polyethylene meet. The latter is the most vulnerable area on the skis and corrective action is needed quickly to prevent the problem from turning into a factory service job.

(5) Make sure the edges are sharp, absolutely square to the bottoms, and undamaged.

(6) Fix (or have your ski shop fix) any damage you discover.

(7) Check your boots for cracks, loose buckles and lost bails, and dry them out and store them in a warm place.

High Dividends

As you can see, there is really not a great deal to maintenance. What skills are required are well worth cultivating. If you think of maintenance in terms of mileage, the dividends it pays in greater skiing pleasure, better and more reliable ski performance, and extra skiing time far outweigh the trouble it takes.

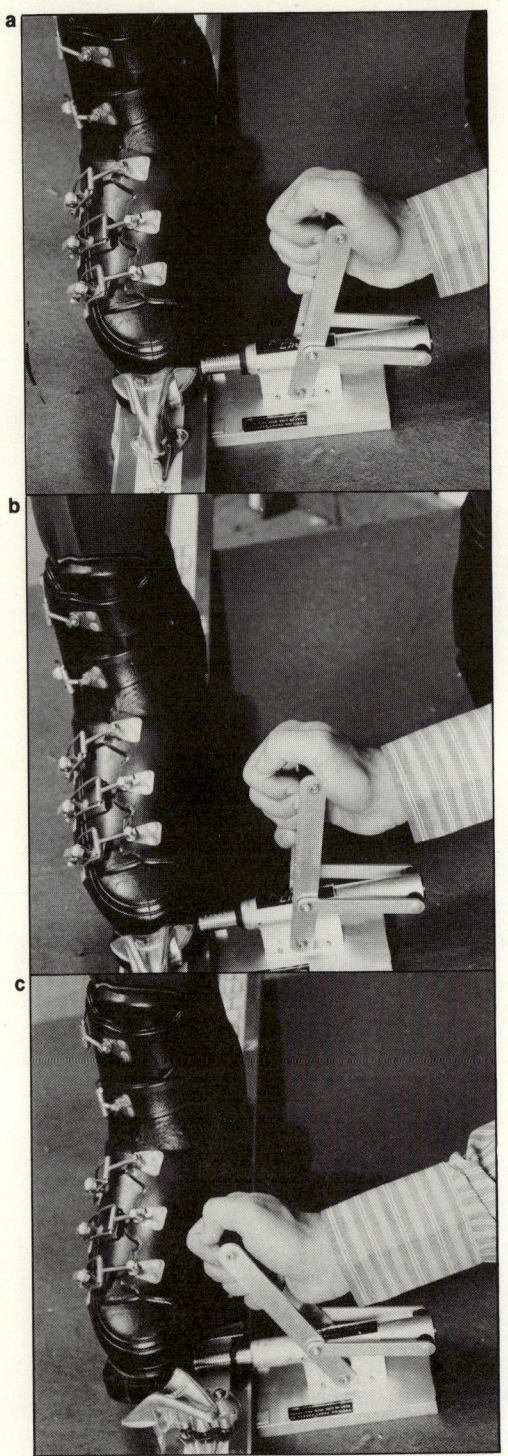

What You Need to Maintain Your Equipment

(1) Selection of waxes for various types of snow conditions.
(2) Cabinet scraper for scraping bottoms.
(3) Wax remover.
(4) Binding tester.
(5) Screwdrivers.
(6) Polyethylene candles.
(7) Surform or coarse file.
(8) File for sharpening edges (six or eight inch mill bastard) or edge sharpener.
(9) Fine sharpening stone and emery paper (medium-coarse and fine).
(10) Spare bails for boot buckles.

The Lipe Release Check is the simplest, most reliable way of making sure your bindings are functioning properly and are correctly adjusted. The spring-loaded plunger of the device is pushed against the sole near the toe of the boot (a) until the boot begins to move (b) and the binding releases (c). A reading is then obtained from the black rubber band around the plunger and the binding setting adjusted according to the table that comes with the device. In addition, the Release Check can tell you if the binding has been mounted correctly and pinpoint other potentially dangerous binding problems.

The Ski Better Book 88

The idea of racing may seem miles above your head, and cross-country, which involves skiing uphill under your own power, too strenous to seem like fun. But like all other types of skiing, both can be geared to your ability and can be valuable aids in sharpening your skiing skills.

Dismiss the notion that racing involves plunging off a steep mountain; it does not. In fact, most better intermediate and advanced skiers would have little trouble handling the terrain on which even the most difficult races are held. It is the way the courses are set and the speeds at which they are run by serious racers that make the difference. I do not want to make light of the raw courage required in international and higher class racing, but most such competitions are, primarily, highly technical tests. Similarly, a race geared to your skills (and there are races even for snowplowers) is a test of your technique and how well you have mastered it.

All races for less than expert skiers are either easy slaloms or giant slaloms, frequently referred to as GS. In slalom, the gates are closer together and there is more emphasis on continuous turning while giant slalom gates are wider with more distance between the gates, and they're set to test the ability to cope with terrain problems.

Running gates is technically the same as free skiing. The real **difference,** however, is that the gates make you turn at a spot and at a speed of the course setter's choosing. And if he is a good one, he will make the course neither so easy that you can simply cruise through it, nor so difficult that it is

Ten
The Uses of Racing and Cross-Country Skiing

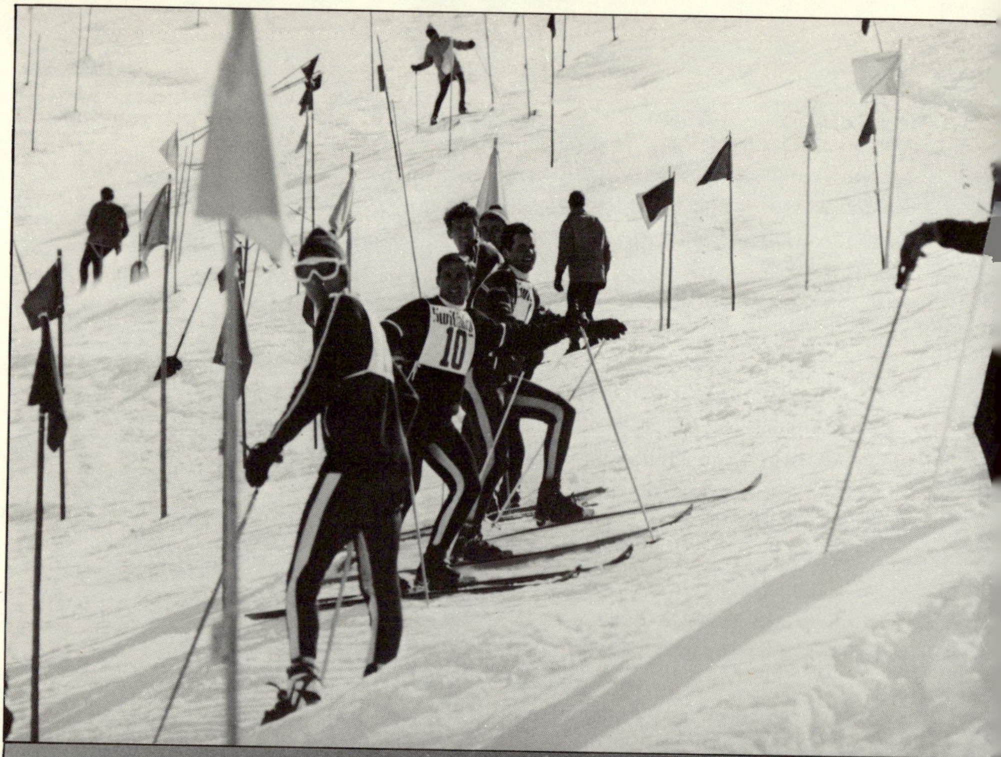
10

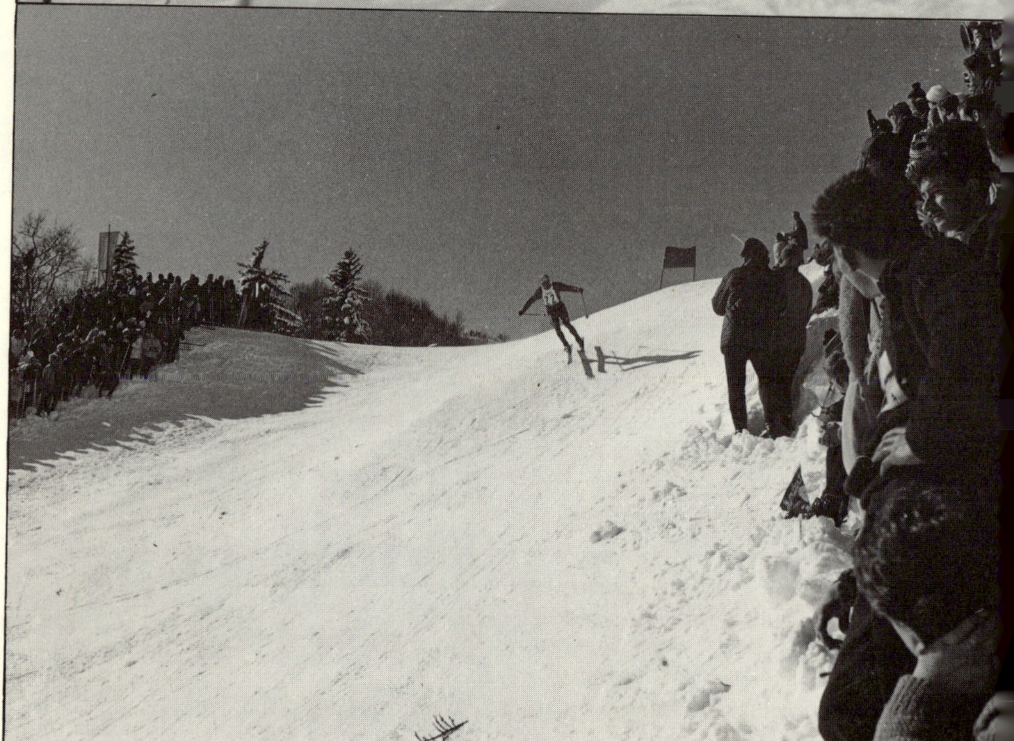

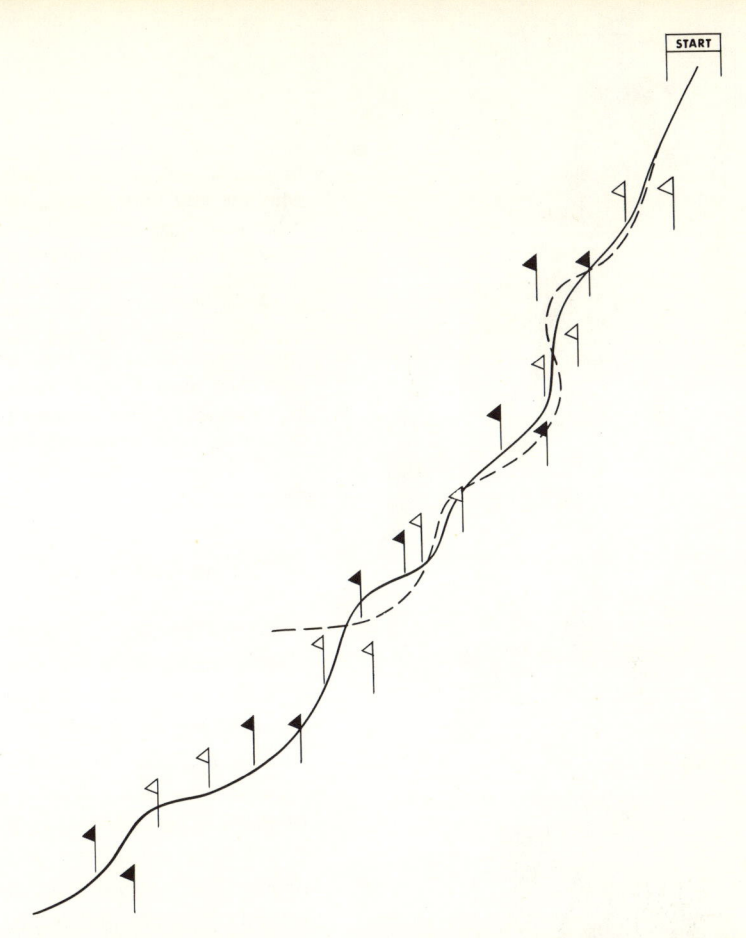

A world-class slalom (left, top) has many gates set close together and in tricky combinations. The gates are much farther apart and on easier terrain for lesser competitors and recreational skiers.

Downhills are nothing for the less-than-expert skier to fool with. They're dangerous, but they're exciting to watch.

This ten-gate course (above) illustrates the need for precision turning in slalom. The solid line indicates the correct line through the course. By waiting a fraction too long to turn—a seemingly minor error—the racer following the broken line not only travels farther, but gets progressively more out of position until he misses the sixth gate completely.

beyond your capability. Faced with this problem, your only options are to ski out of the course or to ski more aggressively. Notice that the first gate in the ten-gate course illustrated is placed in such a way that you have to ski almost straight down the hill. You will have picked up a fair amount of speed before you can start to turn to make it through the second gate.

As you're about to pass through the first gate, you have to turn—NOW!—not so much to make the second gate, but to get through the following ones (solid line). If you fail to turn soon enough, or skid a lot as you turn, it will result in a track through the course indicated by the broken line, and by the fifth gate, you will have slipped so low that you will straddle and miss the next gate.

91 The Uses of Racing and Cross-Country Skiing

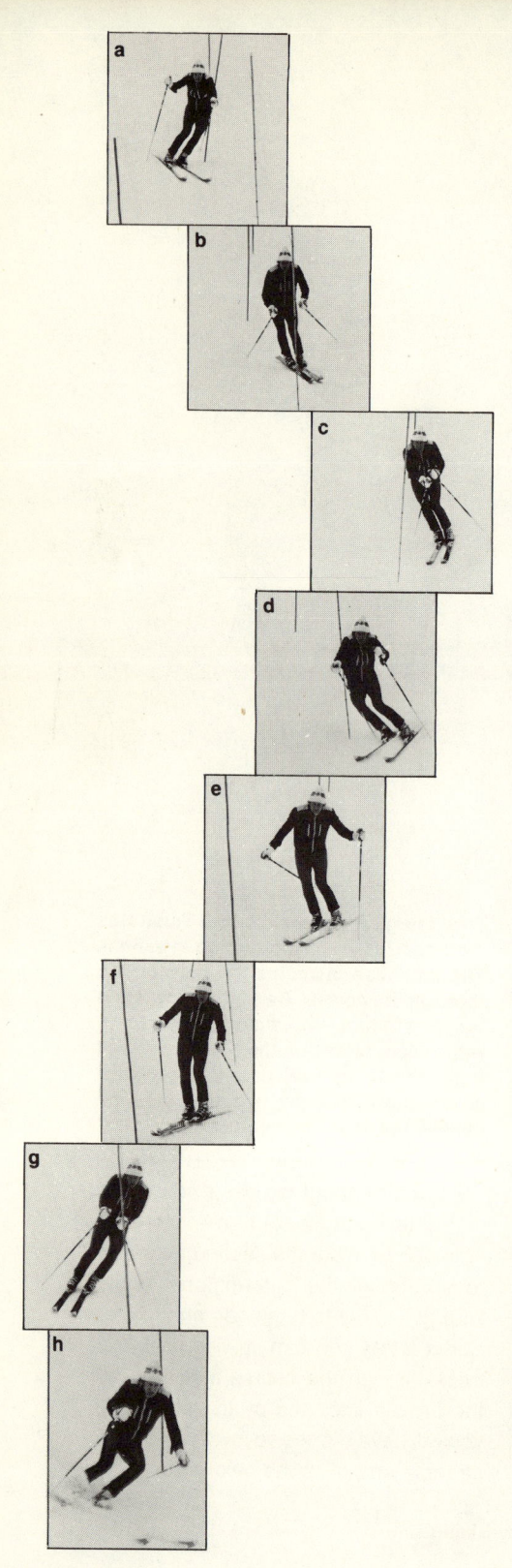

In slalom, forget fine technical details, whether you look stylish, or whatever other problems you think you may have. Concentrate on the gates ahead and scramble and drive as hard as you can to get through. You may be ragged at first, but surprisingly the skis turn without your telling yourself to do this and do that. And after a while, you will forget some of your skiing worries and experience truly spontaneous skiing.

A Classic Demonstration

This little ten-gate course is almost a classic demonstration of the need to look two or three turns ahead and ski aggressively. If you wait until you have passed through one gate to make the turn through the next, or if you try to ease into the turn, rather than really cranking the skis around, you will never make it. Concentrate, instead, on taking closed gates high and getting as close as possible to the inside pole of open gates. It is the best cure for useless body motions (you will have no time for them) and the frequent tendency of skiers to tippy-toe all over the slope *looking* for a place to turn rather than turning.

In slaloms for recreational skiers, the gates are about 12 to 15 feet wide (about two to three ski lengths) and are set into combinations to test the skier's technique in a variety of turning situations. GS gates are wider and there is more distance between them. The emphasis is on handling terrain problems. Downhills, which require careful course preparation, are primarily tests of speed with control gates placed in such a way as to lead the racer over certain classic

The Ski Better Book 92

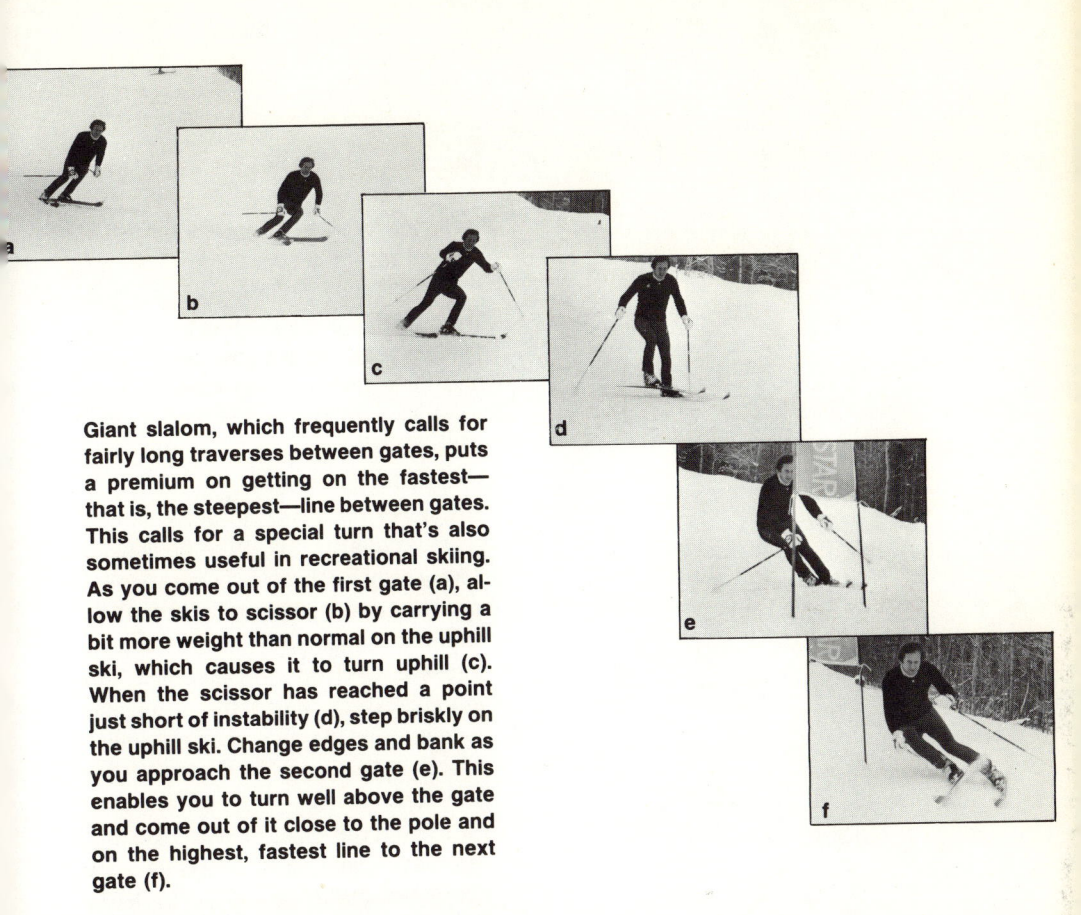

Giant slalom, which frequently calls for fairly long traverses between gates, puts a premium on getting on the fastest—that is, the steepest—line between gates. This calls for a special turn that's also sometimes useful in recreational skiing. As you come out of the first gate (a), allow the skis to scissor (b) by carrying a bit more weight than normal on the uphill ski, which causes it to turn uphill (c). When the scissor has reached a point just short of instability (d), step briskly on the uphill ski. Change edges and bank as you approach the second gate (e). This enables you to turn well above the gate and come out of it close to the pole and on the highest, fastest line to the next gate (f).

downhill terrain (rolls, steep sections, etc.), or to steer him away from obstacles, or to check his speed where there is a danger of its becoming excessive.

Most better ski schools devote some time to running gates in their intermediate and advanced classes, because it is one of the best ways known to reduce self-consciousness. It forces you to think in terms of skiing problems instead of your own. It teaches you precision and makes you more aggressive.

Setting Your Own Course

Whether you are on your own or with friends, you can find at most ski areas a slope tucked away where a course has been set, or poles are available so you can set one.

Setting a course to test the abilities of serious racers is something of an art, but it is not beyond skiers' capabilities. Watch how it is done a few times, then try it yourself. Setting your own course and then running it will sharpen your perception of terrain and snow problems and give you a clearer picture of your skiing capabilities.

It is not necessary to set a formal course, certainly not at the beginning. Simply plant single poles about 15 to 20 feet apart, staying directly in the fall line where the terrain is easy, and coming across the hill where it steepens. As you improve in setting and in running courses, you can then change to two-pole gates and some more challenging gate combinations.

Racing, or at least running gates, is especially useful if ski areas in your vicinity lack challenge and variety. It will provide you with a good measuring stick of your progress and will give you a strong incentive to improve, besides being psychologically satisfying.

An informal, single-pole slalom is easy to set and good practice at areas where there's little variety in terrain. Don't make the course too complicated or difficult, and set it to keep away from obstacles.

The skinny ski movement is burgeoning in this country after having been a Scandinavian specialty for centuries. Some of the touring races—races primarily for recreational skiers who want to see how they stack up—draw skiers in the thousands. Note especially the light-weight equipment, made specifically for the gliding stride that enables the better conditioned practitioners to cover dozens of miles a day almost without effort.

Cross-Country

Cross-country is a sport in its own right. It is technically different from downhill skiing and requires its own special equipment. Very basically, it is walking or running on skis, but the way it is actually practiced involves a special and easily mastered stride called **the diagonal,** which takes maximum advantage of the gliding properties of skis. This enables the proficient skier to cover ground at a rate three or four times faster than walking. Top-flight international cross-country competitors can maintain an average speed of 13 mph for several hours.

Cross-country skiing for recreational purposes is usually called **touring** and is frequently compared to hiking on skis. Personally, I dislike this comparison because it conjures up the notion that cross-country is sort of plodding along. Quite the contrary is true. At its best, cross-country is a rhythmic gliding over the rolling terrain that, in its own way, is as satisfying as downhill skiing.

Special Equipment

The cross-country skier uses equipment specially made for the sport. Skis, boots, poles, and bindings are made as light as possible to minimize the skier's

a **b** **c**

The rhythmic stride and glide can be practiced as a leisurely walk or at a fast competitive clip of up to 15 miles an hour. The poleplant, even more important in touring than in Alpine skiing, is coordinated with the kick to get maximum glide between strides. This particular stride is called the diagonal.

a **b** **c**

For variation, change of pace, or stronger drive, cross-country skiers also use a double-poling stride and may even kick repeatedly with the same leg instead of alternating.

effort and to maximize his freedom of movement. Hence, the skis are narrow and without steel edges and cambered in such a way as to provide forward thrust when the skier kicks off into his stride. The bindings are little more than toe clips that leave the heel free to move up and down. The boots are not much more than track shoes. The poles are about shoulder height so that the drive of the arms can be used to supplement the power of the stride. Clothing is light and roomy since the skier is constantly on the move. Warm-up pants and parka should be taken along in a small knapsack to prevent chilling during stops.

The Secret

Wax is the secret to cross-country skiing and it must be carefully matched to the snow conditions. Skis properly prepared with special cross-country waxes will slip back neither during the kicking phase of the stride nor while climbing. Yet, they will glide readily. This used to be a fairly tricky business, and for racing it still is. But in the last few years, it has been greatly simplified for touring purposes with kits that cover most of the conditions with two or three waxes. There are also skis with special bottoms that do not need wax, but none, so far, glide and climb as well as waxed skis.

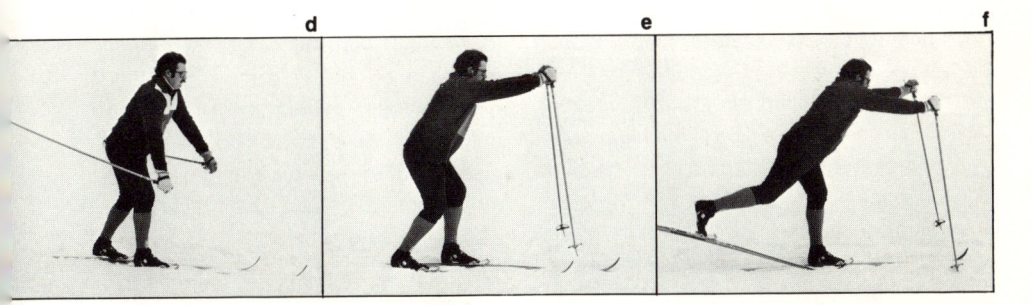

Of what use is cross-country skiing to the downhill skier?

As can be readily imagined, it is an almost ideal means for conditioning. And since the amount of exercise can be readily geared to your needs at any given time, it is one of the most pleasant ways devised of getting into shape. Furthermore, in most northerly sections of the country, there are usually more opportunities to ski cross-country than downhill. You can ski almost anytime or anywhere there is snow on the ground, in a local park or on a golf course, if nothing else is available.

Although maneuvering the edgeless skis is technically quite different (on steep sections of narrow trails, you may have to resort to putting the poles between your legs and sitting on them to remain in control), the experience sharpens your sense of balance. The feeling of where you are on your skis and where the skis are in relation to the snow is keen. With only the toes of the boot fastened to the narrow skis, you will feel quite unstable at first, but that is what makes cross-country so useful. The skis are extremely sensitive and let you know, instantly, when you are out of balance, or if your weight is misplaced.

Note especially that during the kick most of the weight must be on the kicking leg for maximum drive. This requires a constant, subtle adjustment in balance, natural enough when walking or running on firm ground, but more difficult when gliding on skis, especially when you are not skiing on a prepared cross-country track.

There are a number of exercises to improve balance and feeling for the skis

97 The Uses of Racing and Cross-Country Skiing

in downhill skiing, but basically, they are skills that are not so much taught as acquired through experience. Cross-country skiing, where poor balance manifests itself instantly in poor glide and broken rhythm, is one of the best ways to get that experience and to add to your skiing miles.

Ski Mountaineering

There is another kind of touring, frequently called **Alpine** touring because it originated in the European Alps. More accurately called *ski mountaineering,* it is, essentially, skiing in the high mountains where there are no lifts. The climb is made either on foot or with the aid of skins fastened to the bottoms of the skis, allowing them to slide forward but not backward.

Ski mountaineers also use special bindings that leave the heels free to move up and down during the climb and can be locked for the downhill run. The technique is the same as for regular downhill skiing, but you should be proficient in powder and variable snow conditions before attempting anything ambitious.

Ski mountaineering can be extremely risky. The undisturbed snow in the high mountains of the West and in the Alps is notoriously avalanche-prone under certain conditions. Even minor injuries, such as a twisted ankle, can be disastrous when you are far from help. **Never ski alone,** and make sure there is an experienced ski mountaineer in your party.

The risks and effort involved are more than worth it. Climbing a great mountain on skis and then sweeping down its flanks in great smoking arcs is rightly considered to be the ultimate expression of the skiing art, an unforgettable experience, and the reward for becoming a better skier.

In the spring and early summer, when the warm sun has settled the snow in the high mountains and on the glaciers, ski mountaineers come into their own. In Europe, where mountain huts are scattered throughout the Alps, mountaineering is more popular than in this country where, beyond the lift-served areas, you're very much on your own.

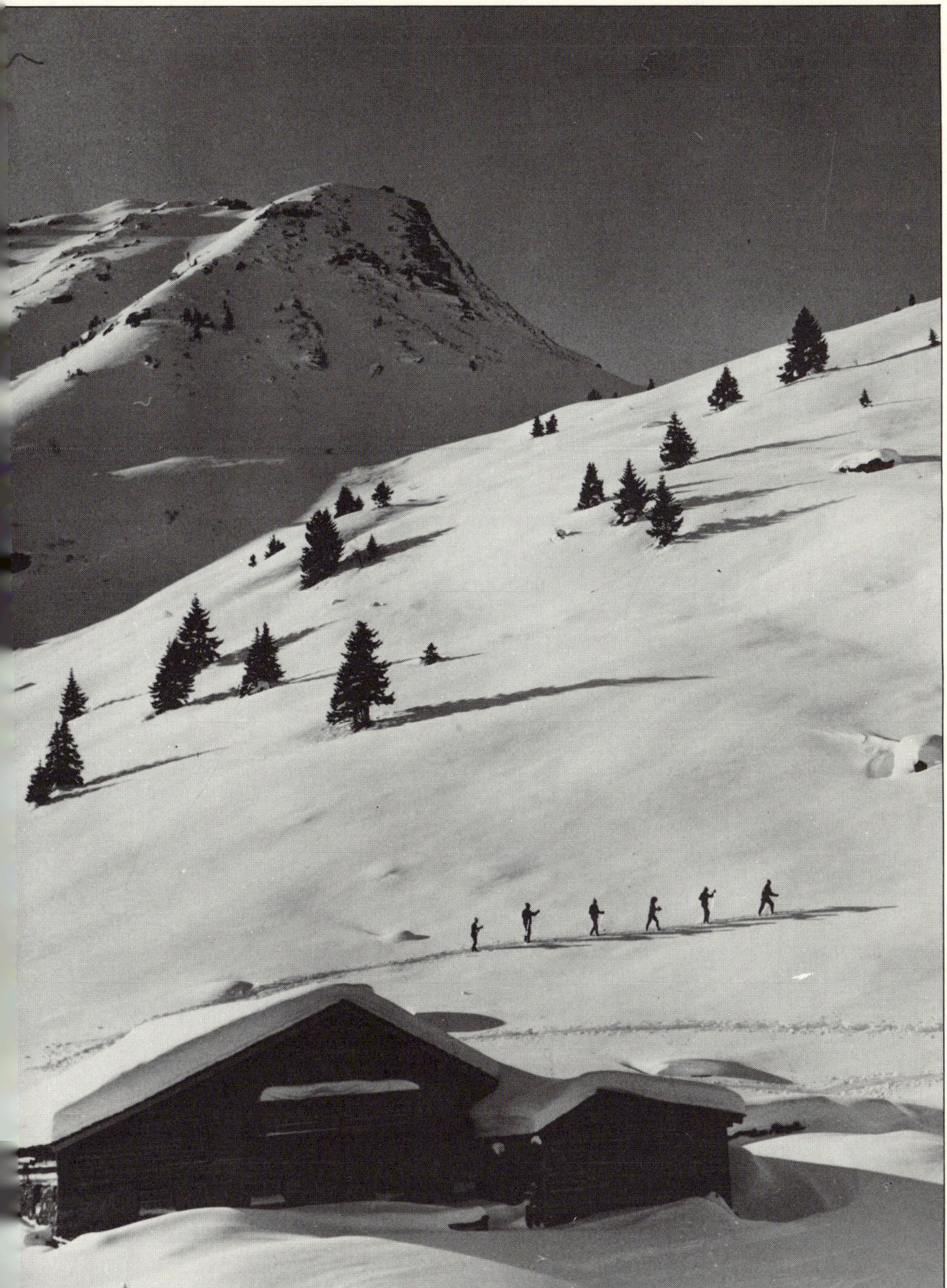

Eleven
If It's White and Slippery, Ski on It!

If some of the statistics about skiers are any indication at all, there are four chances in five that you are not getting nearly enough mileage to become a good skier. Moreover, much of the mileage you do get is, in effect, wasted because a good part of your time spent on skis is used to catch up to where you left off the last time.

Despite some opinion to the contrary, skiing is not an especially difficult sport to learn. What *is* difficult is finding enough time within the relatively short ski season to get the opportunity to learn. Unlike most other sports facilities, ski areas are not standard municipal recreation fare like golf courses and tennis courts. For most Americans, skiing involves some sort of overnight trip, requiring money as well as time, something few can afford to be lavish about.

Saving Grace

If there is a saving grace in this bind, it is that an athletic skill once mastered is rarely forgotten. Millions who have not ridden a bicycle since their early teens take it up again twenty years later. Much the same is true in skiing. You may get a bit rusty, but it does not take long for your reflexes to remember if they have been properly educated.

If you are just learning to ski, or you have decided that this is the year you will get it all together, the first problem you must solve is the time-money bind so that you can learn with a minimum of slippage between sessions.

This immediately raises two questions: What is a good skier? How long does it take to become one?

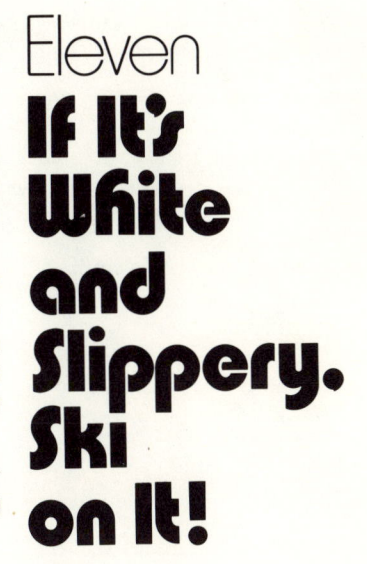

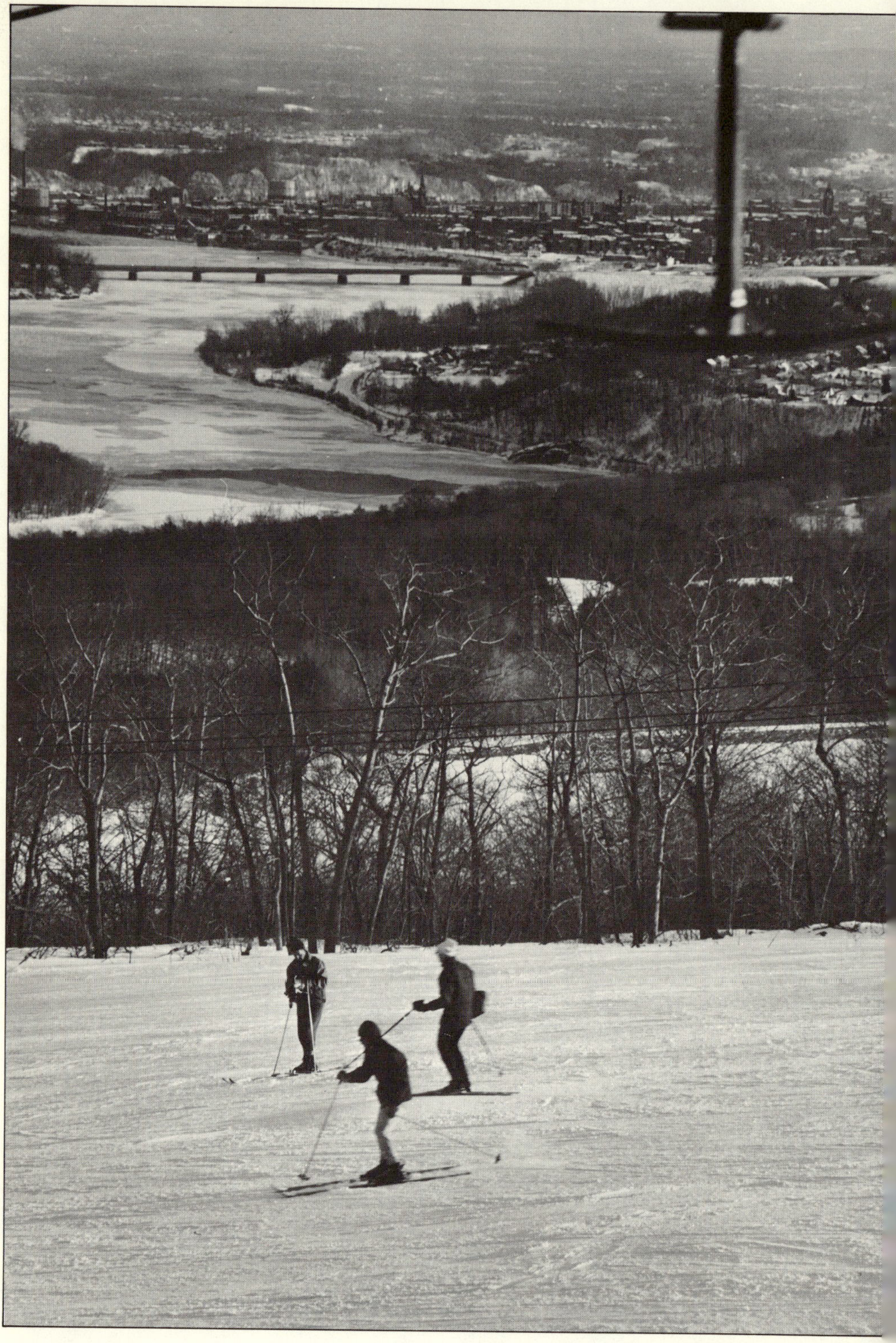

(Above.) Just because an area is small doesn't mean that it can't have character and charm. Although Gray Rocks Inn in Quebec's Laurentians hasn't anything that's remotely terrifying, it has a widespread reputation as one of the best places to go to learn to ski. Excellent accommodations and personal attention make up for any lack of challenging terrain.

(Left.) With the aid of snowmaking machines, ski areas, such as Mt. Tom near Springfield, Massachusetts, are coming closer to metropolitan areas. If there's such an area near you, make the most of it to pile up skiing miles.

Neither can be answered precisely, given the multitude of motivations for skiing and the different rates at which people learn. Usually it takes between twenty and thirty concentrated days on skis to make all but the truly spastic reasonably competent skiers. If you are at all serious about becoming a good skier, try to schedule at least that much time between Thanksgiving and mid-April for skiing.

Time for most skiers is most readily available on weekends, and the holidays during ski season: Thanksgiving, Christmas–New Year's, Washington's Birthday, and Easter at areas with a sufficiently long season. That is a total of forty to fifty days, and theoretically, more than enough time for you to get a good grip on the sport within one season. Unfortunately, these periods are also the time when ski areas are at their very busiest and when prices for lifts, lessons and lodging are at their highest. It will not only cost you more, but you also get a lot less skiing. Although there are many variables, it is safe to say that the cost per skiing mile more than doubles if you ski on weekends and holidays only.

Don't Sacrifice Continuity for Glamor

In contrast, you get more miles for your money if you ski between Monday and Friday, prior to the Christmas holidays, in January, and after the third week in March. Aside from the difficulties in getting away for mid-week skiing, you should be aware that ski conditions can be marginal at the beginning and the end of the season. January, too, tends to alternate thaws with extreme cold in many ski regions. These hazards, however, are frequently overstated and they should not discourage you from

---

Good snow, interesting terrain, and exciting side attractions are not confined to the super-resorts. The U.S. is dotted with about 300 unsung, medium-sized areas like Boise Basin, Idaho, which have all the ingredients to make a first-rate skier out of anyone who's interested in becoming one.

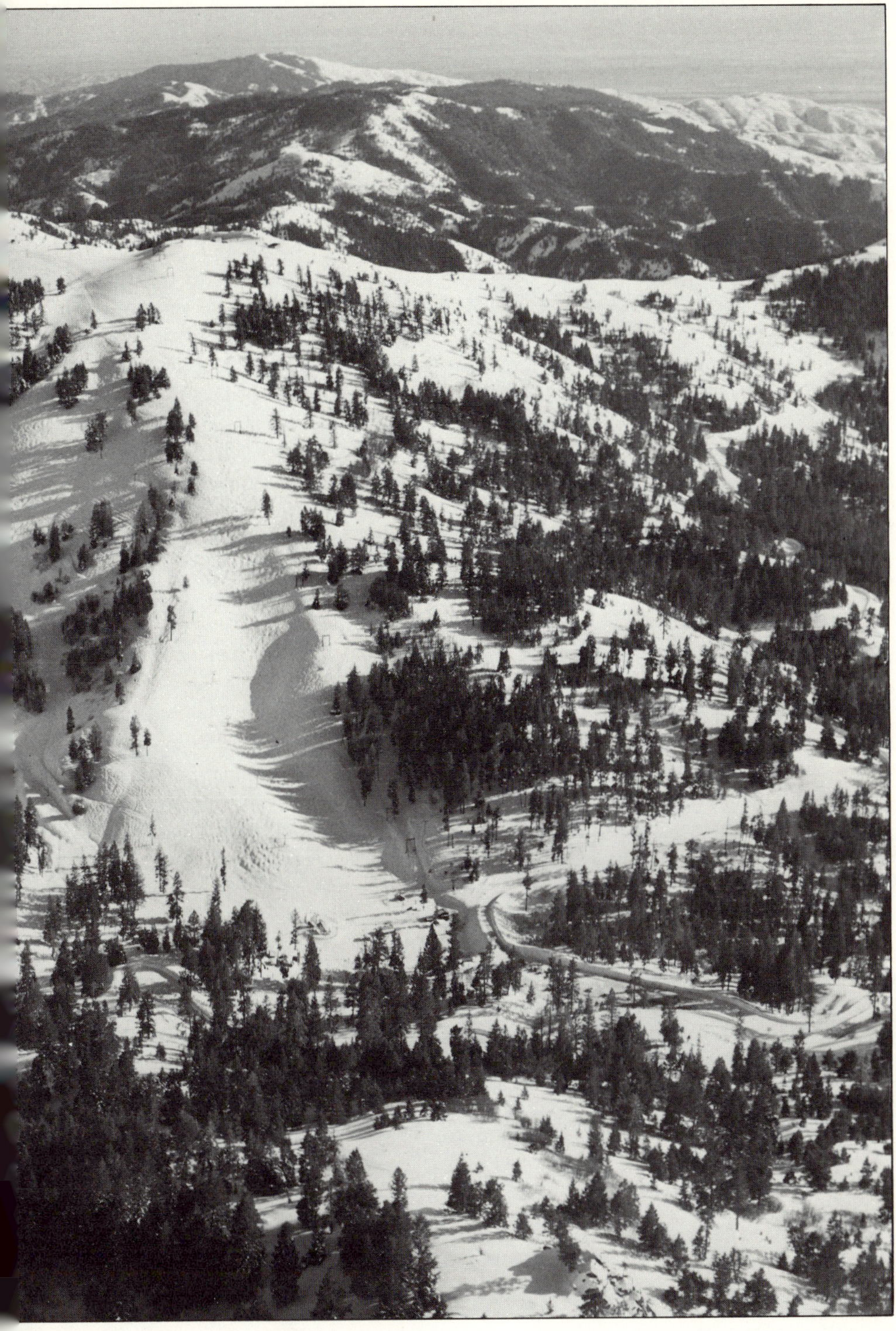

scheduling skiing days during these periods, particularly in late spring, when the weather is balmy and even weekend crowds are minimal. Since the lodges are rarely filled during these periods, last-minute reservations are no problem if your skiing involves an overnight stay away from home.

In planning your season's schedule remember that, even though the snow may be deeper and better at more distant areas, travel costs money. If you go far enough, you will have to pay for lodging and meals as well as gas and oil. Equally important, long weekend trips can be physically exhausting. There is always the chance of encountering icy highways, more nerve-wracking than anything you will encounter on skis. As long as there is a challenge at areas closer to home, do not sacrifice continuity simply for the sake of skiing on a more glamorous mountain.

If there is a ski area within an hour or two of driving time from home, enabling you to return on the same day and to bring lunch along, by all means use it. If it has night skiing, be sure to take advantage of that to by-pass weekend crowds. If you do not have any other choices nearby and plan to do most of your skiing there, check out the cost of a season's pass. It may be cheaper in the long run, although you should know that you do not get your money back if the season is a flop.

Ski Clubs

When the nearest skiing to you requires an overnight stay, you will be tied to a much tighter schedule and it will cost a good deal more. Consequently, truly dedicated skiers try to settle close to ski country.

Ski clubs can be helpful. At the very least, you will be thrown together with like-minded individuals who will share the driving chores and traveling expenses. Many ski clubs are quite elaborate organizations which rent or own ski houses and sponsor charter bus and train trips to leading resorts in the West and Europe. The savings from such an affiliation can be quite substantial, although it does lock you into the group's schedule. But do not give up if you cannot find a club with a timetable of activities that matches yours. Ask friends, check ski shop bulletin boards and newspaper classifieds, and scout around the ski area of your choice for partners to share transportation and lodging expenses.

When weekending and overnighting is unavoidable, as it is for most American skiers, it makes financial sense and will benefit your learning progress to take a ski vacation of at least a week. A week's stay usually costs less for lifts, lessons, and lodging than an equivalent number of weekend days. More important, you get a lot more skiing for your money. Furthermore, seven days of continuous skiing invariably increases your skill and confidence more than the

---

This country's famed resorts, including Vail, Colorado, where President Ford spends his Christmas vacations, are famous for good reasons. They're able to cater to your every whim and offer almost every conceivable type of skiing challenge. For some they may be a bit overwhelming, but you can be sure that you'll not go far wrong.

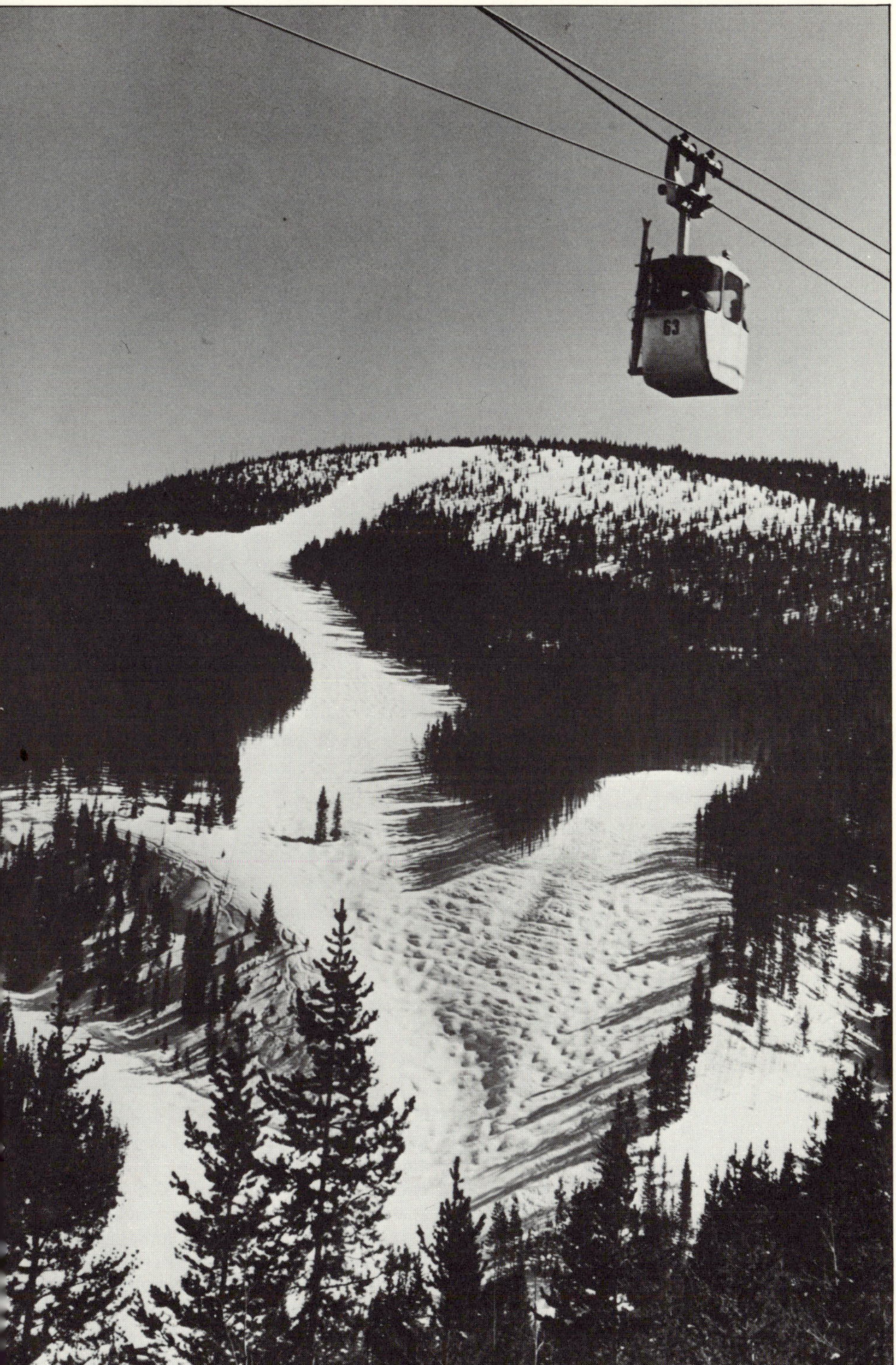
63

same number of days spread out over a month or more.

Ski vacations make sense, even for those who have skiing close to home. For those out of weekending range, vacations are the only answer. A change of scene and challenges adds spice and interest to the sport and gives you some idea of skiing's endless possibilities.

Choosing a Ski Area

Like bananas, ski areas tend to come in bunches. But despite their proximity, few of them are alike. How do you go about picking one, particularly when you are doing so from a distance?

Fortunately, or unfortunately, depending on your point of view, most ski areas put the major emphasis on intermediate terrain. Most skiers fall into that category; hence, ski areas do their best to cater to their needs and it is virtually certain that you will find something suitable for you wherever you choose to go.

This sounds a little simpler than it really is. Many intermediate trails in the East, which tend to be on the narrow side, can turn into expert trails almost overnight when conditions are right for blue ice. In the West, heavy snowfalls can ruin your day unless you know how to ski powder. With modern grooming equipment, these conditions will be temporary. But since every skiing day is valuable, there should be enough variety at your area so that you can continue skiing under adverse conditions without having to go back to the beginner's slope.

Variety of slopes and trails is important in other respects. If your choice is limited and you have to yo-yo the same trail all day long, you may not only get bored, but you probably will not learn much unless you are still at the stage of mastering the basics. This does not mean that an area has to have an elaborate layout for intermediates, but it should have enough moguls, dips, rolls, turns, and variations in pitch so that there is constant challenge and interest.

If you do decide to follow a fairly concentrated improvement program, you will probably outgrow your home area if it is a small one. When skiing begins to seem too simple, when you no longer feel that bite of challenge, it is time to move on to something more demanding and, if nothing suitable is nearby, to think about that ski vacation.

No Shortage of Facilities

You will find no lack of areas at which you can spend your vacation dollars. You will find them listed in the major ski publications, such as *Skiing,* which has a special vacation issue early in the fall, and various skiing guides that are avail-

---

Europe's international resorts are fully the match of the Big Ones in this country and in some respects surpass them. Zermatt with its Matterhorn and miles and miles of open-slope skiing is a favorite of Americans for its unique atmosphere. European ski schools are first-rate, but you'll probably get more out of the Alps after you've accumulated some skiing experience to take advantage of that fabulous terrain.

The Ski Better Book   108

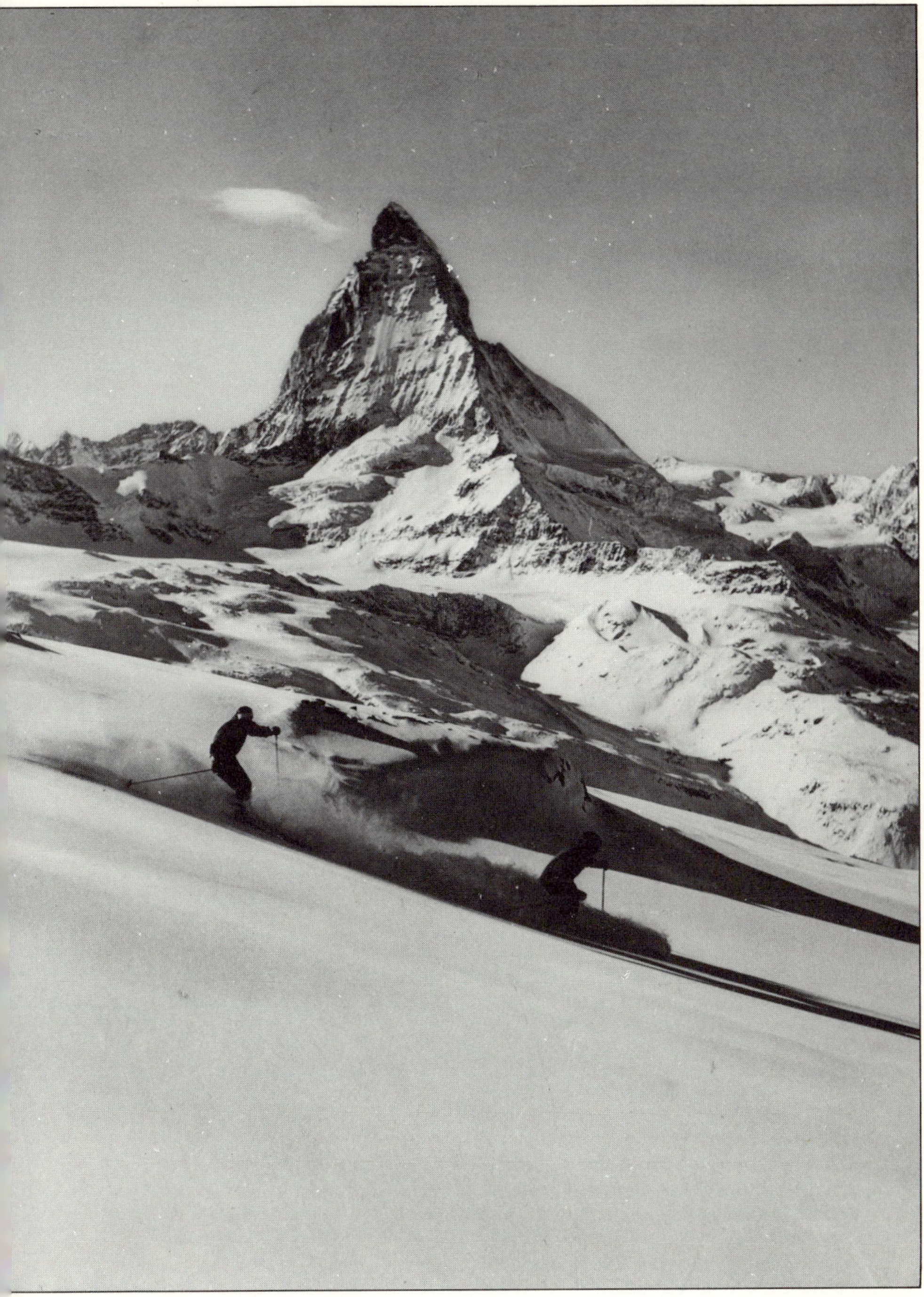

able in book and ski shops. Many areas exhibit at the fall ski shows, which are held in the major cities throughout the country and which give you an opportunity to talk personally with their representatives and to pick up brochures with information on lifts, lessons, lodging, and restaurants.

If there is a weakness in this approach to choosing an area, it is that only a few areas are selected for comprehensive article treatment in each issue of the ski magazines and that the guides tend to be skimpy on details. As for brochures and movies, it is only natural for the areas to put their best foot forward. The skies will always be blue, the trails always quilted with fresh powder, and the fireplace always crackling with warmth and companionship. If you are lucky, very lucky, you will find the conditions as advertised. **Don't count on it!** There have to be some cloudy days if there is going to be snow on the ground.

However, brochures are useful sources of information on costs of lifts, lessons, and lodging, and the various package plans offered. If you are on a tight budget, study these packages, as they offer substantial savings on the prices listed in the other parts of the brochure, particularly during the less busy parts of the season.

A few inches of fluffy powder over a good base makes even inexperienced skiers feel euphoric and heroic. Aspen is noted for this ideal condition, which is why every skiing dreamer wants to settle there. This takes ingenuity and explains why the town has more and better restaurants and livelier and longer after-ski life than any other resort.

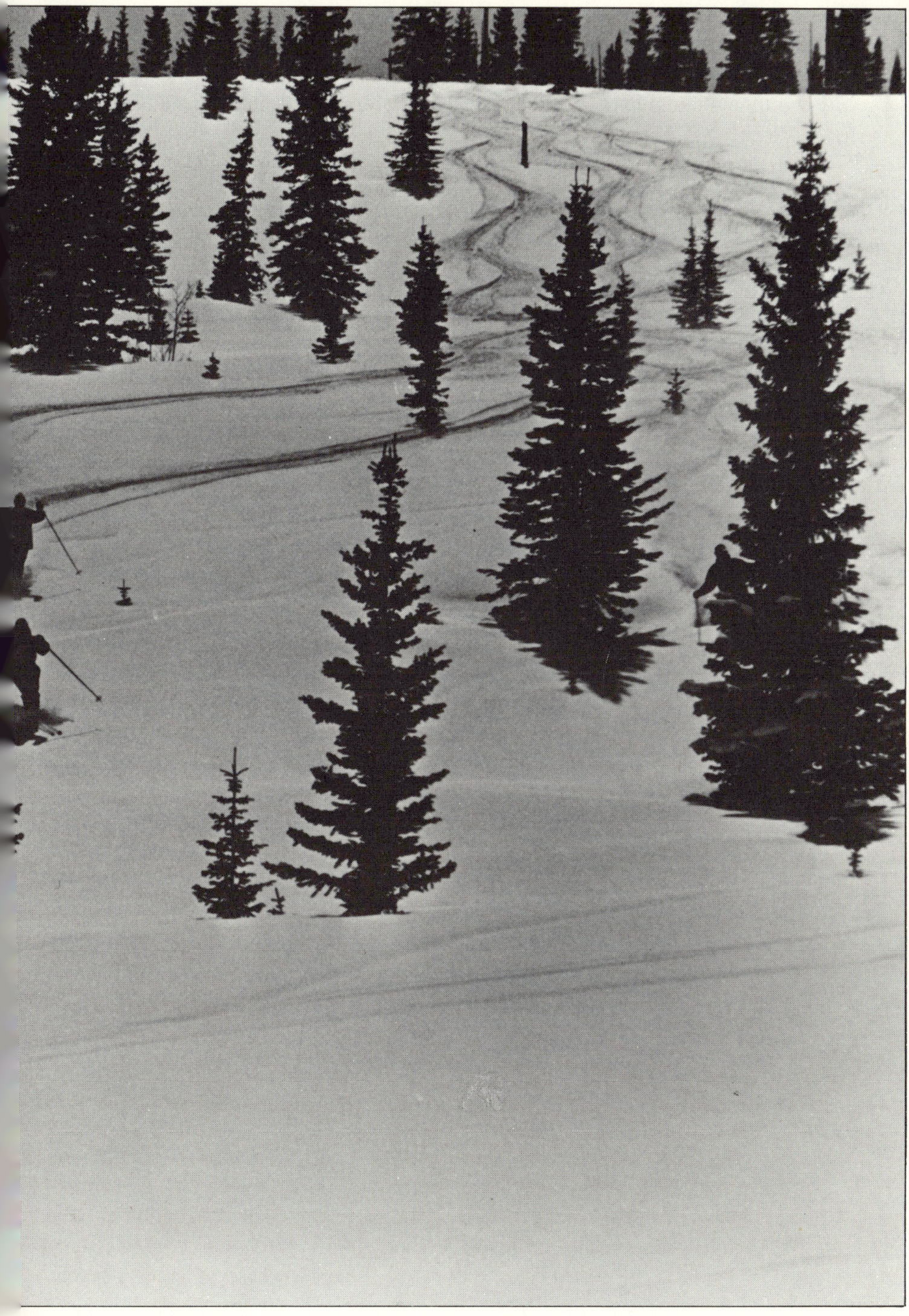

Be sure you know what is *not* included in a package! Most, but not all, western resort lodges operate on the European plan (continental breakfast only); most eastern and midwestern lodges are on a modified American plan (breakfast and dinner).

Decipher the Code

In addition, brochures invariably provide unconscious clues to what you can expect from an area if you can decipher the code. The best clue is the area's vertical rise—the straight-up distance between the bottom of the lowest lift and the top of the highest lift. Areas with less than 1,500 feet of vertical may have their charms, but sustained challenge and long runs are not going to be among them. This does not mean that areas with more than 1,500 feet are automatically difficult, but you are more likely to find truly tough terrain. Remember that monster mountains are few and far between in the United States and Canada.

Since brochure writers try to make the most of an area's assets, they cannot help but give the show away somewhere along the line. Undue emphasis on the ski school, beginner's slopes, and fun trails is a tip-off that the area is on the easy side.

An accent on excitement, high bowls, and deep powder is a good indication that it has more to offer to advanced skiers.

A good trail map can help you confirm your suspicions. It is usually a sign of a good area if the brochure includes such a map.

Skiers' Grapevine

You can double-check your impressions by plugging into the skiers' grapevine, which is probably the best source of unvarnished information. By the nature of the sport, skiers are a well-travelled lot, and there is a very good chance you will find someone who has been where you want to go and is willing to give you his opinions on the place.

It is not necessary to go to one of the major resorts, such as Aspen, Sun Valley, or Stowe, for a vacation. It may not be necessary to travel very far if becoming a better skier is your major objective. All that you need is a mountain or cluster of mountains that have enough challenge and variety to give you an incentive to improve and a good ski school to provide help if needed.

Skiers have a general tendency to overreact to weather and snow reports, but if you are trying to string together twenty to thirty days in a season, you cannot afford to be too fussy. You cannot ignore prevailing weather trends over the various ski regions, but day-to-day reports are relatively meaningless as long as there is reasonably good snow cover. You can ski only on the top few inches anyway.

About the only rule that seems to hold is that high-altitude resorts have more reliable snow conditions than low-altitude areas. February and March usually have the best combination of good snow, good weather, and moderate temperatures. However, in my own experience, I have had superb skiing in various sections of the country, including the much-maligned East, as early as

October and as late as the Fourth of July.

Consequently, I pronounce one of my Cardinal Rules of Skiing: IF IT'S WHITE AND SLIPPERY, SKI ON IT!

Scheduling Your Season

Every skier's circumstances differ in the amount of time and money available, his physical condition, his distance from the nearest skiing, and the way he learns. Consequently, you have to develop your own program, taking all the variables into account. However, some of the following tips may be helpful in laying out your schedule:

Physical conditioning is a major factor in learning to ski. If you are out of shape, you are going to have a tough time, even though gravity does much of the work. If you jog, play tennis, or follow any other acrobatic exercise regularly, you are in good enough shape to ski. But if you have had a lazy summer, you must follow some exercise program to make the most of your days on the hill.

Even if you are in shape, there is invariably a period of adjustment to the particular physical demands of skiing and of the equipment. Taking a day or two at a time in the beginning of the season is probably the best way to get the kinks out of your muscles and the bugs out of your equipment.

Try to gear your schedule to the way and pace you learn. Some of us have to just keep plugging along, some are athletically adept, some have quick response, some need time between sessions to digest the experience, some need drill, etc. Try to set your schedule to mesh with your learning pace and make budget allowances for lessons to help you get over those stages when no improvement seems to be evident.

Better Long-Run Results

Although I have seen quite a few skiers make spectacular progress by concentrating virtually all of their season's skiing into a two-week vacation, one, two, and three-day sessions spread over the course of a season have proved to yield better long-run results. Save that ski vacation for the time when you feel you are near a breakthrough, or, if you have to make long weekend hauls, when you begin to get a bit travel-weary.

If you are uncertain about scheduling, wait until the season starts. After the first few days, you will get a pretty good idea of how you should proceed. In any event, keep in mind that any program has to be geared to your pace of learning and your particular needs. Quite frequently, you will be tempted or urged to ski at areas and on trails at a time that is not of your own choosing. Until you are reasonably sure of your skiing, resist those urges. Don't forget, this is the season when *learning* to ski is your first priority.

Although you should try to stick to a program, do not put yourself into a straitjacket either. Progress may be faster or slower than you expected. Weather conditions and days off may change. So stay loose, allow yourself some latitude, and be prepared for surprises. It is part of the fascination of skiing.

Adaptability, 66
Alpine touring, 98
American Society for Testing and Materials (ASTM), 42
American Teaching Method (ATM), 3, 10
Angulation, 31, 60, 63
Anticipation, 52–53
Aspen, Colorado, 112
Austrian Teaching Method, 2, 3
Avalement, 13

Balance, 13, 27–32; boots and, 31; centrifugal force and, 31; cross-country skiing and, 97–98; edging and, 24, 31–32, 59–63; exercises in, 59–63; functional, 30–31; improving, 28–30; stance, 27–28; in turns, 24, 59–63
Banking, 73
Bindings, 1, 42–45; for cross-country skiing, 95–96; maintenance, 87; selecting, 42–45; for ski mountaineering, 98
Blue ice, 72–73, 80, 108
Boilerplate ice, 72–73
Bonnet, Honoré, 7
Boots, 1, 35–38; balance and, 31; for cross-country skiing, 95–96; design, 14, 23; function, 35–36; height, 36–37; maintenance, 87; rental, 33, 34, 35; stiffness, 36, 37
Brochures, 110, 112

Camber, 23
Carved turns, 24–25, 63–64
Centrifugal force, 15, 31, 64
Clothing, 45, 96
Clubs, 106, 108
Counter-rotation, 54–55
Course setting, 93–94
Cross-country skiing, 89, 95–99

Diagonal, 95
Downhills, 92–93
Down-unweighting, 48

Eastern ski areas, 108, 112–113
Edge change, 21–25, 47, 59–63
Edging, 16–26; balance, 24, 31–32, 59–63; change of direction, 21–25, 47, 59–63; complete reversal, 19; points of emphasis, 26; precise control, 20–21, 24–25; side-slipping, 17–21; skidding, 24–25
Epoxy, 87
Equipment, 33–45; clothing, 45, 96; cross-

Index

country skiing, 95–96; experience and, 33–34; French, 8; season rentals, 33–35. **See also** Bindings; Boots; Poles; Skis
Error analysis, 64–65

Fall line, 15, 71
Fear, 66, 79–82
Files, 85
Foeger, Walter, 5
Freestyling, 58
French racers, 7–8
French Teaching Method, 2, 3
Friction, 15–16, 19

Gates, running, 89–94
Giant slaloms, 89, 92
Gouges, filling in, 87
Graduated Length Method (GLM), 3, 10
Gravity, 14–15, 19

Heel-push, 55
Hotdogging, 58
Hot-waxing, 82, 85, 87, 96–98

Ice, 72–73, 80, 108

Jetting, 53

Killy, Jean-Claude, 8
Knee crank, 51–52

Lateral projection, 72–73

Mileage, 7–10; scheduling, 103–104, 106, 113
Moguls, 71, 108

Non-plate bindings, 42, 43

Parallel turns, 2, 3–5
Pfeiffer, Doug, 5
Physical conditioning, 65–66, 113
Plate-type bindings, 42–43
Poles: for cross-country skiing, 95–96; edge change and, 63; planting, 49–50, 53, 63; selecting, 45
Polyethylene candles, 87

Racing, 89–94
Rasps, 87
Relaxing, 66–67

Rentals, equipment, 33–35, 38–39
Reverse camber, 23, 63
Risk-taking, calculated, 79–82

Schaeffler, Willy, 66
Scheduling, 103–104, 106, 113
Scrapers, 82
Season rentals, 33–35
Short-ski instruction, 5
Shortswing, 2
Sidecut, 22
Sideslipping, 17–21, 80
Skating on the flat exercises, 28
Ski areas, choosing, 106, 108, 110, 112
Ski boots. **See** Boots
Ski clubs, 106, 108
Ski instruction, 1–6, 8–10, 13
Ski mountaineering, 98
Ski Tül, 85
Skidding, 24–25, 63–64
Skiing, 5, 108
Skis, 1, 38–42; body weight and, 34; for cross-country skiing, 95–96; demonstration, 41–42; design, 14, 22–23; friction and, 15–16; length, 40–41; maintenance, 82–88; rental, 33, 34, 38–39; selecting, 39–42; waxing, 82, 85, 87, 96–98
Slaloms, 89, 92
Slope doping, 82
Snow conditions, 72–75; blue ice, 72–73, 80, 108; boilerplate ice, 72–73; deep snow, 73, 75; high-altitude resorts, 112; scheduling and, 104, 106; ski area choice and, 108; ski mountaineering and, 98
Snowplow, 2, 57, 58
Spontaneity, 67
Stance, 27–28
Stanley Surform, 87
Stemmed maneuvers, 2, 3, 57–58
Stowe, Vermont, 112
Sun Valley, Idaho, 112

Taylor, Clif, 5
Terrain, 66, 69–72. **See also** Snow conditions
Touring, 95–98
Trail map, 112
Traverses, 17, 80
Turn initiation, 47–55, 59; anticipation, 52–

53; counter-rotation, 54–55; edge change, 21–25, 47, 59–63; heel-push, 55; jetting, 53; knee crank, 51–52; pole planting, 49–50, 53, 63; turning power, 50–55; unweighting, 47–49, 63, 72–73

Turns, 57–65; balance in, 24, 59–63; banking, 73; basic skills, 58; carved, 24–25, 63–64; centrifugal force and, 15; error detection and correction, 64–65; key movement, 59; parallel, 2, 3–5; sequence of events in, 58–59; ski design and, 22–23; skidding and, 24–25, 63–64; snow conditions and, 72–75; stemmed, 2, 3, 57–58. **See also** Turn initiation

Unweighting, 47–49, 63, 72–73
Up-unweighting, 48

Wax remover, 87
Waxing, 82, 85, 87, 96–98
Weather reports, 112
Weekend skiing, 103–104, 106, 113
Western ski areas, 108, 112
Witherell, Warren, 5